Tucci

A Level Playing Field

Based on the Alain Locke Lectures

A Level
Playing Field

AFRICAN AMERICAN ATHLETES
AND THE REPUBLIC OF SPORTS

Gerald L. Early

HARVARD UNIVERSITY PRESS

Cambridge, Massachusetts, and London, England

2011

Library of Congress Cataloging-in-Publication Data

Early, Gerald Lyn.
A level playing field : African American athletes and the republic
of sports / Gerald L. Early.
p. cm.
Includes bibliographical references.
ISBN 978-0-674-05098-3 (alk. paper)
1. African American athletes—History.   2. Sports—United
States—History.   3. Discrimination in sports—United States—
History.   4. African American athletes—Social conditions.
I. Title.
GV583.E26   2011
796.092'2—dc22   2010047288

Contents

PART II Heroism and the Republic of Sports

Acknowledgments

The chapters that make up Part I of this volume were presented as the Alain Locke Lectures in 2004 at the Du Bois Institute at Harvard University, and I am thankful to Henry Louis Gates and Lawrence Bobo for giving me the opportunity to have such a forum to present some ideas I had about African Americans and sports. Two of the three lectures have been revised for publication: the arguments strengthened and clarified as a service to myself and also to my readers. The chapters, taken together, roughly cover African Americans and sports in the post–World War II era, from Jackie Robinson, Paul Robeson, and the HUAC–House Un-American Activities Committee (the late 1940s and early 1950s) to Curt Flood and his challenge of major league baseball's reserve clause (the late 1960s and early 1970s) to the Donovan McNabb and Rush Limbaugh controversy (the twenty-first century). The chapters have certain thematic linkages that give them unity, more apparent now than when they were delivered as lectures. I would like to thank Lindsay Waters for believing in this project sufficiently to publish these lectures. I am also grateful to the National Humanities Center, where I was the John Hope Franklin Fellow in 2001–2002. It was there that the first draft of the Jackie Robinson essay was written. I am grateful to readers who read this work in the manuscript stage and offered good suggestions for improving it and to my friend, accomplished sports historian Michael McCambridge, for reading and offering incisive criticism of two of the lectures. These readers should share in the credit of whatever is good here; what remains bad is a reflection of my inadequacy and no one else's.

The three chapters in Part II—"American Integration, Black Heroism, and the Meaning of Jackie Robinson," originally published in the *Chronicle of Higher Education* on May 23, 1997; "Performance and Reality: Race, Sports, and the Modern World," from *The Nation*, August 10, 1998; and "Where Have We Gone, Mr. Robinson?" from *Time*, April 12, 2007—constitute my most sustained sports commentary during these years (1992–2008), aside from my service as an on-air analyst for Ken Burns's *Baseball*

(1994) and *Unforgivable Blackness: The Rise and Fall of Jack Johnson* (2005) and for several ESPN and HBO sports documentaries, including features on Bob Gibson, Muhammad Ali, Sonny Liston, and the history of the black athlete. What I liked most about writing the chapters that constitute the second part of this book is that I was permitted to return to the popular essay, which I liked very much, as it was the form of writing that gave me my fame, such as it may be. In short, I was a writer about sports (not a sportswriter) rather than a scholar about sports, and here I felt much more keenly the effect of having read Hemingway, Liebling, Mailer, Bill James, C. L. R. James, and Carlo Rotello, a certain literary aspiration in writing about sports. It is perhaps this distinction that I wish to make between approach and sensibility in delineating the two sections of this book. In the first part, in the lectures, I wanted very much to make a scholar's argument and, in revising the lectures for publication, felt I had as much space as I wished, which allowed me to include lengthy annotations to create a rather grand effect; in the second part of the book I am the writer and thinker, the commentator, if you will, operating within the clear constraints of the magazine piece, limited word counts, and no access to any form of annotation. This distinction is important for the reader in order to understand what each part of the book is trying to achieve and how it is trying to achieve it.

Over the years, I have reviewed many sports books. I enjoy reading sports books, even books about sports that I do not like. Boxing books remain my absolute favorites, followed by baseball books. I could have written more sports essays if I had had the time to do so. The lack of production was not a reflection of my lack of interest. I wrote a few pieces about boxing during this span, but I wrote more about baseball because my appearance in Burns's popular documentary on the sport rather sealed my connection to it. I chose not to include any of my boxing pieces here to give this book a certain sense of unity—all of the chapters are about players engaged in team sports. My sole regret is that I have not written more about professional (American) football, a sport I have always loved and, in recent years through my friendship with sports historian Michael McCambridge, have learned to appreciate even more. The two pieces on Robinson in Part II complement and overlap very nicely with the Robinson chapter that opens this book. It is interesting that I was commissioned to write essays on

Robinson commemorating both the fiftieth and sixtieth anniversaries of his start with the Brooklyn Dodgers—the Burns effect, no doubt, but I am actually rather proud of that; I assume, however, that once the seventieth anniversary rolls around, editors will seek younger and fresher perspectives. I do not think I have anything more to say about Robinson, and it is odd for me to think that when I was in my twenties I swore that I would never write about Robinson at all. I might add that the last Robinson piece (Chapter 6) generated some mild controversy because I said blacks choose not to play baseball, which some people found extraordinary and wanted to recite to me all sorts of "structural" stuff about high Little League fees, lack of green space in black urban communities, and the uninviting atmosphere of mostly white college baseball teams and the like as reasons blacks are excluded from playing baseball. I never found any of these reasons, on close examination, to be especially persuasive, but I was taken by the fact that there seems to be a persistency in this world, both political and intellectual, never to give black people agency except as a sign of rebellion. Otherwise, all of our choices are made by racism. That belief, however well intentioned as a form of analysis, sometimes gives me the willies.

Black people were never that crazy about baseball when it was, back in the 1920s and 1930s, the only professional game in town! *The Nation* essay, which appears as Chapter 5 in this book, complements and overlaps in very useful ways with the Introduction and with aspects of the chapters that make up Part I. I thought that that essay was a rather strangely lyrical, even somewhat elegiac, piece for *The Nation*, but once again I am proud that I was asked to write it. I find it amusing to think that nearly all of the sports pieces I have written during this period were commissioned. I wonder if I would have chosen these subjects myself if I were free to write about anything that interested me about sports. In retrospect, I rather have the feeling of a jazz musician playing, to borrow a phrase, everyone's song but my own.

Finally, I would like to thank my wife and my two daughters who, over the years, have watched on television or attended many sporting events with me, particularly baseball games, even though they do not particularly like sports. They have allowed me to explain sports to them at great length, have supported my passion for particular athletes and teams, have celebrated when my favorites won, and have commiserated with me when they lost.

They have heard all of the arguments in this book rehearsed dozens of times. I am humbled by the fact that they did this because they wanted to share in something that gave me so much pleasure, that made me happy, and that what made me happy made them happy too. In this way they taught me much more than I ever taught them. To paraphrase C. L. R. James, *what do they know of sports who only sports know?*

A Level Playing Field

Introduction

Who'll be my role model
now that my role model is gone?
  —Paul Simon, "You Can Call Me Al"

"NO ATHLETE IS ONLY AN ATHLETE," writes Debra Shogan in her book *The Making of High-Performance Athletes: Discipline, Diversity, and Ethics* (1999), and this is almost self-evidently true. "Despite the detail of sport discipline, athlete identity is not consumed by it. Athletes, like other people, participate in a number of overlapping conflicting disciplines that together produce a distinctive hybrid identity for each person."[1] All high-performance athletes are products of the social and cultural systems that created them, of the systems and ways of life that value their activities and their achievements; further, they are emblems, exemplars, and representations of those systems in ways that virtually no one else is or no one else can be. The "hybridity" of star athletes—their construction as athletes and the intersection of that construction with the other constructions that define them in a number of complex, even conflicted, ways—makes them compelling social figures, both transcendent and constrained. This book is divided into two parts. The first section is comprised of three case studies and, in the second part, commentaries on the significance of the high-performance, hybrid athlete in post-World War II America are offered. Part I, based on a set of lectures, and Part II, composed of previously published non-academic essays, were conceived, taken together, to be an entity, an interlocking statement, a sustained examination of race, high performance athletics, and history.

High-performance athletes are social constructions, as we all are, but they are peculiar in their construction, singular. High-performance athletes are not merely social roles or a collection of habits and customs; they are mythologies. On a certain level, athletes are a special sort of socially constructed mirror that reflects a romanticized version of cultural honor and cultural virtue. Athletes can be heroic and celebrated for their heroism in their performance in the way no artist or worker in another line of work can, for the athlete can symbolize the honor of a group or nation in dramatic, even melodramatic, terms. High-performance athletics is perhaps the most theatrical and emotional form of ritualized honor that we have left in the world. Of course artists and other nonathletic types have become national and group heroes,[2] but a great high-performance athlete can more easily be elevated to this role because he or she is usually young, and youth has an intensely charismatic appeal to most people; he or she has obtained a standard of excellence that is self-evident and objectively measurable and has had to achieve greatness by performing under enormous public and competitive pressure.

I examine African American athletes in this book because they offer an instructive and a complex view, a compelling ironical perspective of athletic honor as they represent, in part, a group that was historically considered socially without honor: they are, arguably, the most imposing hybrid figures in American sports. A certain ambiguity clouds the reputation of African American athletes even today; they cannot seem to shake their social degradation. What else could explain a book such as William Rhoden's *Forty Million Dollar Slaves: The Rise, Fall, and Redemption of the Black Athlete*, which argues that despite the fact that blacks make up the majority of players in the National Football League and the National Basketball Association and are "a significant minority in Major League Baseball" (how significant seems a burning question at the moment, as some are arguing that American blacks are underrepresented in baseball as their percentage in the sport has dropped over the last thirty years), "access to power and control has been choked off. The power relationship that had been established on the plantation has not changed, even if the circumstances around it have."[3] That the field of dreams that constitutes American sports could be construed as a plantation of menial forced labor might strike some readers as bizarrely inapt and other readers as militantly Marxist. It is a strange thing to say that something people freely choose to do, are paid for, and derive much personal satisfaction and acclaim from is a form of slavery! Whatever the case, since at least the 1960s, several noted African American athletes and writers have interpreted the black athlete as some sort of glorified slave. And for an even longer period, since at least the time of slavery itself, blacks have been a bit ambivalent about sports and playing games. In Chapter 5 (an essay about African Americans and sports originally written for the periodical *The Nation*) I discuss the slavery simile. I do not find the slavery simile to be especially persuasive as an analytical depiction of blacks and American sports. After all, the opposite of slavery is freedom, and if high-performance athletics represents a form of slavery, then what would free labor in sports, or freedom in sports, or no sports at all look or be like? Would it look like Luddite nonprofessionalism and non-competition, sports as pure, "uncorrupted" play? Non-private ownership of team franchises? The end of leagues themselves? The end of all commercial licensing and profit taking? Athletics controlled completely by the athletes themselves, without coaches, managers, or trainers? The end of sports as a form of consumerism? The slavery analogy only works well if one can argue compellingly that blacks are being coerced into sports, that black athletes symbolize involuntary servitude. That is not a wholly unjustified or fatuous argument to make if one considers and is offended by the conclusion to Charles Murray and Richard Herrnstein's *The Bell Curve: Intelligence and Class Structure in American Life* (1995), or if one is persuaded by John Hoberman's argument in *Darwin's Athletes*, but in both instances the entire issue of the role of blacks, especially black males, in American society may be improperly framed: blacks do not represent unfree labor but, rather, corralled and controlled, channeled if you will, labor, if one is insistent on a Marxist reading. On the one hand, because of the stigma that African Americans bear as socially inferior people, the ghost of slavery frequently haunts virtually any physical labor they may choose to perform.[4] On the other hand, it must be remembered that the money, the fame, the nature of the competition, and the idealized discipline associated with sports represented not slavery but freedom to African Americans, a considerable form of achievement and recognition, indeed, a form of power in their exertions as trained athletes. Moreover, as high performance athletics has developed economically in this country, the highly skilled black athlete has had increasing access to a number of important institutions and industries, far more than the average black person: colleges and universities; professional sports franchises and leagues; television, radio, and Internet sports broadcasts; and the sporting goods, advertising, and nutrition industries. What I do find most fascinating is how attractive the idea of sports as slavery has been for blacks in considering how to interpret the construction of the black athlete, the most fabled and admired of all African Americans in popular culture. In this regard, it must be remembered that many blacks have always been suspicious of the success of other blacks, especially their success in popular culture, which, seemingly, slavery has indelibly stained: this may explain why many black musicians, actors, and dancers are dismissed by members of their own group as "minstrels" if they appear in work that the audience, rightly or wrongly, thinks is stereotypic or degrading, rather much like calling high-performance black athletes "slaves" because the audience they entertain is largely white. As I have said elsewhere, popular culture has been an enthralling trap from which blacks have never been able to escape with their image intact or completely under their own control. African American pop-culture figures, especially athletes, simultaneously make the most captivating role models and the most disturbing. They represent ambition and the virtue of discipline while they, seemingly, make nothing worthy of serious respect.

To understand more fully black athletes and their meaning, it is important to know that sports are different from other forms of popular culture. The public sees athletics as distinct from art and entertainment, although sports can be artistic to many people and are doubtless entertaining to the millions who follow, obsessively, the fortunes of teams and individual athletes. Allen R. Sanderson of the Department of Economics at the University of Chicago posed some of the contradictions in how we see American sports in relation to other aspects of popular culture in his online column "The Puzzling Economics of Sports," posted on the Library of Economics and Liberty website at http://www.econlib.org/library/Columns/2004/Sandersononsports.html. Sanderson writes frequently about the economics of sports for popular publications, and the views he expresses here summarize in a useful and simple fashion the unique position of sports in American popular culture. Professor Sanderson says that "no one complains" about the high salaries of famous actors but that people do complain about the high salaries of professional athletes. This is not quite true, but generally the high salaries of some athletes cause a greater concern for the public at large and generate more anguish about the worth of the person or the worth of what he or she does than expressed about other figures in popular culture. Of course, not all high-performance athletes are extravagantly paid, and some of the complaints of American audiences are probably related to the fact that a good deal of the salary increase that has occurred in American sports in the last thirty or forty years has been the result of union activism and labor unrest in the major spectator sports. During that time work stoppages, lockouts, or strikes have occurred in the three major American professional team sports, baseball (Major League Baseball), basketball (National Basketball Association), and football (National Football League), as well as in professional hockey (National Hockey League), a sport less identified with the United States. Strikes occur among other workers in popular culture, but they do not seem to cause the public as much distress as they do in sports.

Illegal payments to amateur athletes, mostly those who are in college, are a source not only of debate and concern (whether collegiate athletes should be paid is a common topic) but of punishment handed down by regulatory bodies such as the National Collegiate Athletic Association (NCAA) that can severely affect a college's athletic program. In part, people are apt to complain about the high pay of athletes because they have long accepted the romantic, upper-class idea that money corrupts sports and that athletes ought to be inspired by the love of their sport and the spirit of competition and not driven by money, as if high-performance athletics was just another form of work. On the other hand, what makes high-performance athletes the fascinating aristocracy they are for the general public is the fact that many of them make extraordinary sums of money and are able to live seemingly fantasy lives as a reward for their work. Glamor is certainly one aspect of sports that attracts African American boys, much to the unease of some scholars.[5]

Professor Sanderson has identified one important distinction between sports and the rest of popular culture. Here is another: No one complains, Sanderson said, when actors get cosmetic surgery "to improve their competitive advantage," but many were outraged when it was revealed that baseball star Barry Bonds used steroids.[6] Although these acts are not quite the same, Sanderson's observation about what makes sports distinct in this regard is sound. To be sure, cosmetic surgery will not improve an actor's ability to act, but steroids may improve an athlete's ability to perform, and this difference is crucial in understanding how the public responds to a stripper getting breast implants and a bicyclist using human growth hormones and testosterone. The public thinks that the actor's cosmetic surgery is a form of vanity but that use of so-called performance enhancing drugs is a form of cheating and corruption. It is not simply unnatural; it is dishonorable. Yet both the athlete and the actor are trying to prolong their careers by defying aging, and both are doing something that the public considers unnatural. The stakes are higher in sports because the athlete represents something natural (an actor's trade, by definition, is artifice, a pretense)— and in today's highly technological society, there is a virtual mania for the "natural" as something life giving and virtuous—but what is meant by unnatural and natural is not especially clear. Unnatural and natural seem to be at times mere value judgments or expressions of fear we have about how modern life seems to have distanced human beings from nature.[7]

Steroid use is simply an expression of the pressure on the modern athlete to represent progress, to best the performances of older athletes, to exceed old boundaries, and to provide a grander spectacle of human aspiration and accomplishment. Indeed, so fierce is the need for ever greater achievement that, to the public's mind, the ethical dilemma for the modern athlete is usually formulated as either meeting the demands of the sport (and thus using drugs to increase performance levels) or following the rules and not using drugs (making it more difficult for an athlete to be competitive, especially against athletes who use drugs and whose drug use is not detected, since the demand for undetectable performance-enhancing drugs, which are not difficult to create, is very high). However, it must be remembered that athletes indulge many "unnatural" or cruel, punishing practices in order to be successful. The use of performance-enhancing drugs is one in an assortment of such acts. An interesting question is why the focus is on steroids instead of other common customs—from oddball dieting and weight loss to the illegal use of medications to heal injuries to blood doping—that athletes use to gain an edge? The public's need for high-performance athletes to serve as fantasy figures and to have sports not seem endlessly repetitious by having athletes attain new heights of achievement, in part fuels the use of performance-enhancing drugs. But it is not just the public's demand for spectacle; commercial interests that undergird sports also drive the demand for an ever spiraling form of excellence as a form of pressure to keep the high performance athlete from shirking or giving too many routine performances or acting as though winning and losing does not matter. The intense competitive nature of sports, which, too, the public prizes for its drama, as an example of a true meritocracy, and for showing the mettle of the athlete also fuels the use of these drugs. Finally, the commercial and corporate interests that invest in sports and wish a return on their investment inadvertently encourage drug use as well by creating exhaustingly long seasons or tournaments of play. So how athletes wish to improve themselves or prolong their careers is an ethical question of a different sort than it is for actors or rock musicians.

Professor Sanderson also suggests, as do many others, such as sports scholar Allen Guttmann,[8] that because sports are capable of objective measurement and other popular cultural entertainments are not, that that may make a significant difference in the public's mind. The only quantitative or objective measurement used for movies, music, or other forms of popular culture is how much money the individual makes, that is, how well he or she "sells." High-performance athletes are also measured by how much money they make or how much money and attendance their sport attracts, but athletes also perform in a way that is measured and quantified.

How many goals does a soccer player make? How fast does a track star run? How many home runs does a baseball player hit? How many rebounds does a basketball center make? How many strokes did a golfer need to play a round? How many major tournaments can a tennis player win? All of these things can be counted. There is nothing quantifiable in this way that can lead one person to say definitively that the movie *Bend It Like Beckham* is better than *Rocky* or *A League of Their Own* or some other movie about sports. There is nothing quantifiable that can lead one person to say that *Citizen Kane* is unquestionably a better movie than *The Seventh Seal* or that Bruce Springsteen's songs are better than Irving Berlin's or Paul McCartney's. One does not count camera angles or edits in movies or the number of chords or key changes used to write a song as a sign that one is better than another.[9] For African Americans, to be involved in something where performance was clearly quantifiable was an advantage, in that it made it possible for what they did to be understood *impartially*. Professor Sanderson shows in all of his points taken together—in a simple, hardly new, but persuasive way—that sports and athletes are seen differently from the rest of popular culture. Why? In part because of the

unique intersection of sports and science, especially in the development of rational training for
the athlete and in the rise of medical treatment to
quickly repair his or her injuries; in part because
the athlete is a uniquely symbolic being who is able
to represent an institution, a city, or a country; and
in part because sports uniquely combine certainty
(statistics and data) and uncertainty (the fact that
the outcome of sporting contests can never be consistently predicted, as sports unfold live and with no
preset ending) into a heroic narrative of action.

To return to the beginning, the social and political
significance of sports in America and in the world
proves the assertion that no athlete is merely an
athlete. What Professor Shogan meant was that athletes bring to their endeavors what they are not just
as symbols but also as human beings. They shape
their efforts as much as they are shaped by them.
Athletes bring to the sports they perform their tem-
peraments, their politics, their beliefs, their values,
and their psychological and emotional needs. They
may also bring a tendency to rebel against the very
sports ideology that makes their profession possible.
(Professor Shogan poses the example of the obsessed
black basketball adolescent who uses his hard-won

skills to create a "cool pose" of being an outlaw, of being opposed to the very values that his skills are meant to endorse.) Clearly, high-performance athletes are a class in themselves. People who do sports on this level share much in common as personality types. But they are also individuals, diverse and distinct. Nearly all of them are employees. They work for someone else, and no matter how much money these athletes make, they are not as rich as the people who pay them. Even though it is a metaphor that is often used as a compliment for a dominant athletic performance, athletes are not "machines," not automatons, nor should the intensity of competition reduce them to that. Ironically, what dehumanizes the athlete is the very thing we most admire about athletics: merit. Merit is so pure in high-performance athletics that only the best athletes survive, no matter who they are. Athletics is such a perfect thresher that everything social seems subordinate or irrelevant or a form of adversity that the athlete has to overcome. On the one hand, we pretend that only the making of the athlete matters, but of course this is not true in the end. What athletes are, both socially and individually, has a great deal to do with how we respond to them. Heavyweight champion Jack Johnson elicited one response from the white American society in which he performed his work, Joe Louis another, and Muhammad Ali and Floyd Patterson still another. Athletes have families and sex lives. They are not just social constructions or social projections of our needs for the purity of ideals. They are conflicted social entities, messy social animals.

From the post-modernist perspective, if we accept as a given that high-performance athletics as an ideology, originating largely in imperial England, is something that was invented by white heterosexual males and projected or esteemed in some romanticized way those particular social dimensions (that is, whiteness, heterosexuality, and masculinity), then what happens when someone who does not represent one of those dimensions—a new kind of hybridity, as Professor Shogan would put it—is injected into the world of high-performance sports? Is the greatest revolution to occur in popular culture in the world of sports in this era of late capitalism where we see the steady erosion of those dimensions as the defining social qualities of high-performance sports? For now people who are not white, not heterosexual, and not men are major figures in the world of sports. But are these athletes who are not white, not heterosexual, and not male being subsumed or universalized by the whiteness, maleness, and masculinity of sports, or are they instead subverting or re-imaging them? In short, has the democratization of sports, the growing cosmopolitan nature of major sports, in fact challenged the methods and ideology of making athletes and of how they are used? Are we, in some vital ways, witnessing today the deconstruction of sports? What is a sport, and is the sheer proliferation of sports destabilizing what they are not simply by over-extending an industry, but by re-positing and reformulating two essential questions: What are sports? And, how does the high performance athlete function as an identity in the modern world? People are attracted to high-performance sports not simply as a means of expression or as a means of making a living but also because of the very way that one is made a high-performance athlete, and the status that that confers is appealing. It must be remembered that part of the status that accrues to the high-performance athlete is connected to how one is trained and shaped to be an athlete, this lyrical, stylized being of sheer willpower and grace, a prisoner and an auteur of the mystique of the regimen, one might say, combining sacrifice with inner-directed zeal and an almost unbearable single-mindedness. The grandeur of the great athlete is so near a god yet so much a lily of the field, a natural wonder of irrelevance, a specimen of glory and a distortion of indulgence. Is the high-performance athlete something magnificent or merely a mistake? It is certainly not my contention that this small book answers these questions. Rather, it is my hope that the book provides a context for considering aspects of these questions in relation to the hybridity of race and the American sports star, specifically how African American athletes have affected the idea of what it means to be an American and what it means to belong to this society and to represent it in a way that other African Americans cannot.

PART I

Leveling the Playing Field

I

When Worlds Collide:
Jackie Robinson, Paul Robeson,
Harry Truman, and the Korean War

*I didn't know everything I should have known
about the cold war.*
        —Brooklyn Dodgers baseball star Jackie
        Robinson, speaking years later about his
        HUAC testimony

BROOKLYN DODGERS second baseman Jackie
Robinson woke up at 5:30 A.M. on Monday morning, July 18, 1949, to catch an early plane to Washington, D.C., where he was to testify before the House
Un-American Activities Committee (HUAC) at 10
that morning.[1] He was to testify on the subject of
black loyalty or, put another way, on how attached
black Americans felt to a country where they had
been methodically and thoroughly excluded from
its centers of power and ruthlessly persecuted for

the color of their skin. How did Robinson wind up having to do this? In April 1949, singer/actor, former collegiate and professional football player, and noted communist sympathizer Paul Robeson, along with two thousand delegates from fifty nations, attended the Congress of the World Partisans of Peace in Paris, a leftist gathering fraught with tension as the cold war had escalated over the last few years since World War II. American officials were calling Robinson to answer what Robeson had said to this gathering in Paris. It was no ordinary time; rather, it was a crisis moment for the American racial caste system, an extraordinary moment for the United States as the leader of something called the Free World.

Almost immediately after World War II the cold war struggle between the United States and the Soviet Union began to escalate. In most respects this was inevitable, as both America and Russia were expansionist powers with opposing ideologies, neither took the United Nations seriously as a place to settle disputes but only as an international forum to be politicized, and both essentially chose to pursue the geopolitical approach of "spheres of influence" as a way of neutralizing each other as a threat. The 1946–1949 civil war in Greece, in which thousands of Greek leftists and rightists savagely killed each other in what many consider the start of the cold war, pitted the Soviet Union against the United States, as each supported opposing factions. President Harry Truman, speaking to a joint session of Congress in March 1947, "spoke in sweeping, apocalyptic terms of communism as an insidious world menace that lovers of freedom must struggle against at all times and on all fronts" in an effort to gain popular support for backing a corrupt, brutal Greek regime.[2] For the Americans communism had replaced fascism as the new international evil. "A faint odor of fascism emanated from the reactionary Greek government" that America backed, the first of many instances in the cold war when a bad government was supported because the alternative seemed even worse.[3] The United States also provided aid to Turkey to hold off the pressure that the Soviet Union was applying against Turkey to its north. The U.S.-led Berlin airlift to thwart the Soviet blockade of Berlin that occurred in 1948 and did not end until the spring of 1949 was, in some ways, an even more troubling standoff between the United States and the Soviet Union. The split between Soviet-backed North Korea and U.S.-backed South Korea became official in 1948 (which would be the basis of a shooting war in 1950 that directly involved American troops), the same year of the Alger Hiss case (which made the career of Republican California Congressman Richard Nixon), where editor Whittaker Chambers testified before the HUAC that Hiss, a State Department official, had been a Soviet spy and made the public think that the government might be riddled with communists, especially so after Hiss was convicted of perjury in 1950, the same year Senator Joseph McCarthy became a demagogic force for anti-communism by heightening the fear of the enemy "burrowing from within." Many in the United States felt threatened both from without and within by a rigid, emotionless, tightly programmed enemy that lied ruthlessly and hated "freedom." In 1948 Gallup found that 77 percent of Americans felt that there would be another war within ten years, and 43 percent thought it would happen in three or four years. In 1949 Gallup found that 70 percent of Americans opposed their country making a formal pledge not to use the atomic bomb in a first strike.[4] On September 24, just two months after Robinson's testimony, the United States would announce to the public that the Soviet Union had successfully tested its first atomic bomb, constructed, in part, on information supplied by American spies, and in October, the Communist Party of China would announce their victory by declaring that henceforth their country was to be known as the People's Republic of China;—the question "Who lost China?" would echo accusingly in American diplomatic circles for years.

It could be argued that the cold war began on March 12, 1947, when Truman announced to a joint session of Congress his containment policy, designed to make the United States not simply an antagonist to the Soviet Union but to represent America as a role-model state. America was not to be merely a counterforce but a counterexample: open instead of secretive (like the Soviets), forthright instead of duplicitous, encouraging dissent instead of iron conformity, fair instead of partial, and decisive instead of merely coercive.[5] If America had any especial weakness in its attempt to be the role-model state, it was its race problem. It had just concluded fighting a war against fascism, racism, and ethnic genocide with a racially segregated military, among whose leadership it was generally believed that blacks did not make either good combat soldiers or good officers, an irony not lost on a good deal of America's leadership, its allies, and its enemies, and certainly not lost at all on most African Americans. "America has its Achilles heel and . . . the heel is quite black," a Greek newspaper of the period proclaimed.[6] How was America prepared to define the nature of its leadership in regard to its race problem, and what was it to do with its black citizens in this new age of international engagement? America had to create a new liberal narrative denouncing white supremacy as in any way informing its policies either domestically or abroad if it wanted the moral stature to denounce the Soviet Union in this age of the decline of European colonialism.

Paul Robeson was probably among the closest that black Americans came to having among their ranks a true Renaissance or representative man. Born in New Jersey in 1898, Robeson not only excelled academically, earning a bachelor's degree from Rutgers University with Phi Beta Kappa honors (he was not a straight-A student by any means, but he did earn a solid overall B average) and a law degree from Columbia University, but he was also one of the finest collegiate athletes of his time, lettering in football, basketball, track and field, and baseball. He paid for his law education by playing professional football. He was known for his powerful bass-baritone voice, which gave him distinction as an orator. He became a noted singer of Negro spirituals and folk songs, was featured on Broadway in plays by Eugene O'Neill and Shakespeare (*Othello*), and also appeared in several feature films, including *Body and Soul*, by African American director Oscar Michaeux, and *Sanders of the River*, directed by Zoltan Korda. (Korda would later direct a young Sidney Poitier, a great admirer of Robeson, in the 1951 version of *Cry, the Beloved Country*.) Robeson's films were never especially satisfactory from either an artistic or a political point of view, and after 1942, frustrated by his roles, he ceased to appear in them.[7] Robeson, always outspoken about racism and colonialism, became particularly so after his first visit to the Soviet Union in 1934. He opposed South African apartheid, the fascists in the Spanish civil war, and management in nearly any labor dispute. He became increasingly enamored of Russia during World War II and of Africa and negritude as he became more interested in African affairs; in so doing he became, increasingly, an object of concern for the U.S. government and even for mainstream civil rights organizations such as the National Association for the Advancement of Colored People (NAACP), which saw his radical politics as a threat. After World War II both the U.S.

government and anti-communist black leaders became strange bedfellows in a campaign to discredit Robeson.

And so it was that the charismatic, uncompromising Robeson, a compelling anti-American presence at a strikingly tense time in world history, as the Soviets and Americans waged ideological and proxy war, said or allegedly said in Paris, among other things, that the wealth of the United States had been built "on the backs of the white workers from Europe . . . and on the backs of millions of blacks. . . . And we are resolved to share it equally among our children. And we shall not put up with any hysterical raving that urges us to make war on anyone. Our will to fight for peace is strong. We shall not make war on anyone. We shall not make war on the Soviet Union."[8] The Associated Press, in reporting the speech, quoted Robeson:

> We colonial peoples have contributed to the building of the United States and are determined to share in its wealth. We denounce the policy of the United States government, which is similar to that of Hitler and Goebbels. . . . It is unthinkable that American Negroes would go to war on behalf of those who have oppressed us for

generations against a country [the Soviet Union] which in one generation has raised our people to the full dignity of mankind. . . . [9]

Clearly the second statement was at least as incendiary as the first, and maybe more so. But neither was going to go over very well in the United States of 1949, particularly if uttered by a black. Roger Kahn, in his account of Robinson's testimony before the HUAC, writes about a speech Robeson gave in Harlem on June 19, 1949, in which he said, "I love the Negro people from whom I spring. . . . Yes, suffering people the world over—in the way I intensely love the Soviet Union. We do not want to die in vain anymore on foreign battlefields for Wall Street and the greedy supporters of domestic fascism. If we must die, let it be in Mississippi or Georgia."[10] (The last sentence echoes the famous poem by Jamaican writer Claude McKay, "If We Must Die," written in response to the terrible race riots of 1919 and read by Winston Churchill before the U.S. Congress in the early days of the Second World War as a rallying cry for support against the Nazis. Kahn noted that the following day all thirty-seven of the Hearst newspapers ran an identical editorial headlined "An Undesirable Citizen," castigating

Robeson.) Robeson's speech was delivered at a welcome home rally given in Robeson's honor by the Council on African Affairs and was held at the Rockland Palace. About forty-five hundred people attended, half of them white. This would only seem to have fanned the flames of the controversy, which was probably Robeson's intention, as he threw down the gauntlet that he was not going to be intimidated by the United States or by mainstream black leaders who did not like his radicalism: "And I defied—and today I defy—any part of an insolent, dominating America, however powerful; I defy any errand boy, Uncle Toms of the Negro people, to challenge my Americanism because by word and deed I challenge this vicious system to the death.[11] What a travesty is this supposed leadership of a great people! And in this historic time, when their people need them most. How Sojourner Truth, Harriet Tubman, Frederick Douglass must be turning in their graves at this spectacle of a craven, fawning, despicable leadership." One of his most telling observations about American Negroes and their leadership was "They're not afraid of their radicals who point out the awful, indefensible truth of our degradation and exploitation."[12]

Martin Duberman, Robeson's biographer, notes that even if Robeson had said in Paris what the Associated Press said he had said, it would not have been the first time a prominent black would have questioned black participation in American foreign wars.[13] He gives the example of black labor leader and socialist A. Philip Randolph's opposition to World War II and black participation in it.[14] The problem here is that Randolph never opposed World War II. As Randolph said late in his life in commenting on the Vietnam War while it was still raging, "I have always been opposed to wars in principle—though, as in the case of World War II, I am able to support those that are vital to the survival of our democratic institutions."[15] Randolph opposed black participation in World War I. However, Duberman is surprised that the contemporary press treated Robeson's words as if a prominent black had never said anything of the like before—but he should not have been surprised. To be sure, the political situation for blacks at the end of World War I and World War II bore some similarities: intense concern on the part of the government about black disloyalty and radicalism—socialism, black nationalism, and Bolshevism—and vigorous measures to stamp out the latter, the belief that blacks were not effective as combat soldiers and could not be trusted to execute commands on the field of battle.[16] The major difference, though, was that white supremacy was still a viable and defensible political belief and practice in 1919, an unbowed hegemony, whereas it was clearly discredited by the late 1940s. Its loss of legitimacy as a social and political philosophy that informed the structure of institutions cast the entire race question and the government's relationship to it in a different light.

There is also a significant difference in A. Philip Randolph, a name little known outside of the black American community, where he was a powerful and respected leader, and a relatively small circle of political radicals saying that blacks should not fight in World War I in black or socialist publications or at labor union or political gatherings than a Paul Robeson, well known among both blacks and whites, saying what he supposedly said before a large international gathering during the escalation of the cold war. The American government and the white mainstream press would have been doing Randolph a favor by publicizing his remarks widely, as they doubtless realized. Moreover, Duberman takes the remarks a bit out of their historical context. Randolph led the March on Washington movement back in 1941 to not only force the government to desegregate defense industry hiring but also to desegregate the army. If Roosevelt did not comply, then Randolph threatened a march on Washington, throwing out the number of ten thousand blacks converging on the nation's capitol, although the popularity of the idea grew as Randolph campaigned for it, and he probably would have attracted in excess of twenty-five thousand blacks and perhaps even the one hundred thousand he was calling for if he had actually held the march.[17] The thought of such a march in segregated Washington terrified Roosevelt, so he issued Executive Order 8802 in the summer of 1941, which established the Fair Employment Practices Commission and discouraged, to some degree, though by no means came close to eliminating, racially biased hiring in the defense industry. Roosevelt did not integrate the military, did not even really consider doing such a thing. A world war was raging, and America's entry was only a matter of time; Roosevelt asked himself a pressing question: What if whites objected to fighting in an integrated military? How could he wage war with such internal dissension in his own armed forces? Randolph did not bother to press the issue during the war because, as his biographer Jervis Anderson stated, Randolph felt that "in arousing public feeling—black feeling, at any rate—against the military, [it] might tend to embarrass the nation's war effort."[18] Anderson might have added that Randolph would have virtually stood alone among black leaders if he had pressed a civil disobedience campaign against the military during the war. The last thing the vast majority of black leaders wanted was for the black population to be viewed as disloyal.

Randolph, however, revived his campaign to integrate the armed services after the Second World War. In 1947, the same year that Jackie Robinson began his career with the Brooklyn Dodgers, playing first base for the team on opening day in April, a peacetime draft bill was passed by Congress that contained no mention of segregation in the military. Randolph and Grant Reynolds formed the League for Nonviolent Civil Disobedience against Military Segregation by early 1948, which advocated that black men resist the draft. On March 22, 1948, Randolph, with a number of other black leaders, met with Truman at the White House. Among those invited was Lester Granger, head of the National Urban League. At the meeting, Randolph told Truman, "Mr. President, after making several trips around the country, I can tell you that the mood among Negroes of this country is that they will never bear arms again until all forms of bias and discrimination are abolished."[19] Truman did not like being told this. Randolph's statement certainly bears some similarity to what Robeson said, but it is different in several respects. There is no mention of the Soviet Union, or of a particular disinclination on the part of blacks to fight against that country.[20] Randolph is also implying in his statement that if discrimination in the military were abolished, then blacks would fight. There is no mention in Randolph's statement of any larger issues such as colonialism or larger concerns about racism in other institutional forms. Randolph, being a socialist, union organizer, and man of broad political awareness, may have been thinking about such things, but he did not hinge his civil disobedience campaign against the military on them. It was simply presented as a trade: get rid of segregation in the military and blacks will serve. That is fundamentally different from either version of Robeson's statement.[21]

But Truman had been thinking about desegregation of the military before this meeting with Randolph and the other black leaders. On December 5, 1946, nearly a year and a half before the meeting with Randolph, Truman had issued Executive Order 9808, which established the creation of the President's Committee on Civil Rights. The committee's report was issued in October 1947, entitled *To Secure These Rights*, a line taken from the Declaration of Independence. *To Secure These Rights* was a scathing critique of racism and discrimination in the United States, as the report outlined the four freedoms that it thought "essential to the well-being of the individual and to the progress of society":[22] the right to safety and security of the person; the right to citizenship and its privileges; the right to freedom of conscience and expression; and the right to equality of opportunity. These are the ideological cornerstones of the post-World War II civil rights reformist movement and anti-racist, anti-communist liberalism. Here is what the report said about segregation and the military:

> Underlying the theory of compulsory wartime military service in a democratic state is the principle that every citizen, regardless of his station in life, must assist in the defense of the nation when its security is threatened. Despite the discrimination which they encounter in so

many fields, minority group members have time and again met this responsibility. Moreover, since equality in military service assumes great importance as a symbol of democratic goals, minorities have regarded it not only as a duty but as a right.

Yet the record shows that the members of several minorities, fighting and dying for the survival of the nation in which they met bitter prejudice, found that there was discrimination against them even as they fell in battle. Prejudice in any area is an ugly, undemocratic phenomenon; in the armed services, where all men run the risk of death, it is particularly repugnant.[23]

One of the defenses used by military leaders who opposed the integration of the armed services was that the military should not be used for social experimentation and social engineering, for that would damage morale and lessen efficiency. This defense might be called the standard appeal to institutional conservatism, protecting the integrity of how the institution currently conducts its business as the best possible way that it can conduct its business. The report proposed just the opposite:

During the last war we and our allies, with varying but undeniable success, found that the military services can be used to educate citizens on a broad range of social and political problems. The war experience brought to our attention a laboratory in which we may prove that the majority and minorities of our population can train and work and fight side by side in cooperation and harmony. We should not hesitate to take full advantage of this opportunity.[24]

So Truman's committee had strenuously endorsed, several months before Randolph's meeting with the president, the idea of integrating the military. (Truman himself, in 1940, while still a U.S. senator, a stump Democratic stem-winder before the National Colored Democratic Association, especially praised the Negro's service in America's wars: "That the Negro is entitled to every right under the law is sometimes contested on the very weak grounds that he had no worthy part in American history. Turn to your histories then, and you will see the record of patriotism the colored man has written for himself in the pages of our Nation's development. The first American Negro to give up his life for our country's liberty was Crispus Attucks who was shot down in the Boston massacre of 1770."[25] The linkage here between military service and the claim of full citizenship is plain.[26]) It would not have been likely that Truman put together the group, gave them their charge, received their findings, and intended to do nothing about them. (Truman had permitted his attorney general, Tom Clark, on September 26, 1946, to file federal charges against the South Carolina sheriff Lynwood Lanier Shull, who had, in February 1946, so brutalized returning African American army veteran Sergeant Isaac Woodard that the soldier was permanently blinded, one of the most infamous of the cases of racial violence inflicted upon returning black veterans that so moved Truman that he formed his Civil Rights Committee as a result. This response is all the more unusual because Truman grew up with typical white Southern views of blacks, was strongly opposed to social equality between the races, and used racial slurs while in the White House. The filing of federal charges in such an instance of racial violence was unheard of.[27]) Truman gave his most symbolic race speech on June 29, 1947, a nationally broadcast address to the NAACP, the first president to speak to the venerable civil rights organization, at the Lincoln Memorial, where African

American singer Marian Anderson had famously performed on Easter Sunday 1939 after the Daughters of the American Revolution refused to have her perform at Constitution Hall. Here Truman announced his support of civil rights and underscored his anticipation for the report of his Civil Rights Committee. On February 2, 1948, nearly a month after his State of the Union speech, Truman sent a special message to Congress on civil rights, the first president to do so, having received the report from his Civil Rights Committee a few months earlier. He not only reiterated the four freedoms outlined in the report but also recommended the establishment of a permanent Civil Rights Commission and a Fair Employment Practice Commission (which had existed under Roosevelt's Executive Order 8802) and federal protection from lynching. In a sense, therefore, *To Secure These Rights* virtually ensured that the military would be integrated, that it was, in part, an administrative pretext for it. *To Secure These Rights* was meant to redefine the American narrative in light of anti-racist liberalism, relegitimatizing American institutions and cleansing them of the taint of white supremacy.

So Robeson gave his Paris speech nine months after Truman issued in July 1948 Executive Order

9981, which integrated the military, and a little more than a year after Randolph threatened resistance to the draft if the military was not integrated. Robeson's remarks were fraught with more complexity and potential disruption of a delicate reform than perhaps is commonly conceived by those looking back at his remarks. What he said could, in fact, threaten the mainstream liberal, anti-racism reformist movement that Truman's government supported by bringing down upon it all of the wrath and racist paranoia of the cold war. What, indeed, was black loyalty? Was it to support the country despite being mistreated by it? That is probably, at least, a fairly decent shorthand of one version of it. Was black loyalty a political necessity for a country that supported white supremacy but, as a result of World War II, now needed to incorporate African Americans into the civil society because white supremacy was no longer a tenable consensus philosophy? Was black loyalty needed now in a way that it was not after World War I, as an expression of legitimation for an American institution and not simply as something compelled by white hegemony? Whatever it was it was essential for mainstream, anti-racist liberalism to assume that black loyalty existed if Truman's committee was to succeed in its push for integration. Of course black loyalty was important to the Southern conservative as well, its antecedents dating back to slavery and the idea of the loyal black slave, which was what, after all, Uncle Tom, the most mythic slave in American culture, was (although in the end, he did defy Simon Legree, who killed him, a point largely forgotten by most people who probably have never read Harriet Beecher Stowe's 1852 novel anyway). Like the black and white liberals of the 1940s, Booker T. Washington made use of the idea of black loyalty in his famous 1895 Atlanta Exposition speech: the type of black loyalty that comforted white Southerners. It seemed important to the white Southern conservative mind that the African American, no matter how mistreated, could not be moved to disloyalty.[28]

That may explain why Georgia Democrat John S. Wood, chairman of the HUAC, convened a special hearing in mid-July 1949 on black loyalty (officially it was simply to give blacks an opportunity to offer their views contrary to Robeson's), and among the people he subpoenaed was Robinson. In effect what we have here are two competing forms of black loyalty—as a political expression and as a political symbol, the liberal anti-racist version where black civic virtue is blacks' almost martyr-like devotion to fight for a country that mistreats them and the Southern, conservative view that they, possessing a deferential temperament, are predisposed to being loyal to the country, because they are predisposed to being loyal to whites in a child-like way. The tug-of-war was between whether black loyalty would legitimate anti-racist liberalism or the old order of white supremacy. Underneath all of this was a secret fear that blacks might potentially be disloyal. Arnold Rampersad mentions in his biography of Robinson that "[an] informal poll of five hundred white Americans revealed a distrust of black American loyalty and patriotism."[29] In any case, for Robeson, blacks did not have to prove their loyalty in order to be worthy of full citizenship. To have the issue even framed in that way, as both the liberals and the conservatives framed it, was itself a sign of weakness of a black leadership that refused to reassert and redefine the issue but, rather, accepted the way it had been defined for them. For Robeson, the issue was why blacks had been denied their full citizenship to begin with, and that denial, whatever may have caused it, was certainly not based on their loyalty.

In 1949 Jackie Robinson was the most famous black person in the country. (He was also, at the time of his HUAC testimony, the best hitter in the National League, with a .360 batting average.) Indeed, he was among the half dozen most famous Americans, black or white, of his time. In late 1945 the Brooklyn Dodgers signed Robinson, the first black man under contract to play with a major league team in the twentieth century. He had played the previous season—1945—before signing with Brooklyn with the Kansas City Monarchs of the Negro leagues. In the film of Robinson's life, *The Jackie Robinson Story*, released in 1950, which starred Robinson playing himself, when Robinson signed with the Dodgers, it is referred to as signing with "organized baseball," a term despised by people associated with the Negro leagues. Mentioning it to the late Negro leaguer Buck O'Neill would produce a frown. Effa Manley, part of the husband and wife team that owned the Newark Eagles of the Negro leagues, thought that the term was no accident but that it was meant to belittle black baseball and to enable major league clubs to pretend that no legal niceties called contracts existed in that "disorganized" realm. (Robinson and Manley would go at it with competing versions of life in the Negro leagues in the late 1940s and early 1950s.)[30] Robinson enjoyed a great season in the minor leagues with the

Montreal Royals in 1946. He joined the Dodgers in 1947 and won Rookie of the Year honors. His best year in baseball would be 1949, when he would win the Most Valuable Player Award. Robinson wound up leading the National League in batting average and stolen bases. He was second in doubles and triples and third in runs scored. Interestingly, despite hitting only 16 home runs, Robinson drove in 124, one more than St. Louis Cardinals outfielder Stan Musial, who hit 36 home runs, and only three fewer than Pittsburgh Pirates outfielder Ralph Kiner, who hit an astonishing 54 home runs.

But 1949 was also Robinson's year of liberation. According to Branch Rickey, known as the Mahatma by sportswriters, the Dodgers executive who signed Robinson and who pushed for integration: "For three years [that was the agreement] this boy was to turn the other cheek. He did, day after day, until he had no other to turn. They were both beat off. There were slight slip-ups on occasion in that first year in Montreal."[31]

Robinson had agreed to ignore all slights, insults, and abuses that he endured on the playing field during his first three years as a professional ballplayer in the white leagues. This generated, naturally, a certain public sympathy, as Robinson did, indeed, endure much abuse, and he did not have a natural or an easy camaraderie with most of his white team- mates. He became almost a perfect Gandhi-like figure of sacrifice and forbearance, and he created the paradigm for how integration was to proceed in the United States in the 1950s and early 1960s—the Noble Negro who, through his nobility, a mystical product of his American heritage of suffering but enduring devotion to the foundational principles of American life, legitimates white institutions as he integrates them. As the *New York Times* put it in 1950, "The going wasn't easy. Jackie Robinson met open or covert hostility with the spirit of a gallant gentleman. He kept his temper, he kept his poise and he played good baseball. Now he has won his battle. No fan threatens to riot, no player threat- ens to go on strike when Jackie Robinson, or any one of several Negroes, takes the field."[32] This is the Robinson that is always remembered when his career is reexamined today. He is almost always sentimentalized.

But it must be remembered that Robinson played major league baseball with the Dodgers for ten years, only two of which were under this agreement. (The agreement also included the year in Montreal.) So for most of his career as a big league ballplayer, Robinson did not act in any sort of self-sacrificing, nonviolent way. He was a tough, almost chip-on-the-shoulder player, a particularly aggressive athlete who usually took umbrage at the least slight or unfairness he felt on the field. He understood that high-performance sports were about intimidation, and he was not about to be intimidated.[33] Also, Robinson was not entirely alone for those first three years. Larry Doby joined the Cleveland Indians of the American League as its first black player the same year Robinson joined the Dodgers.[34] The St. Louis Browns signed Hank Thompson and Willard Brown from the Kansas City Monarchs and Piper Davis from the Birmingham Black Barons, although Davis never was added to the Browns roster. Thompson and Brown failed with the Browns, probably because they were so ostracized by their white teammates, because they played for such a poor team, and because they themselves were not the best-suited personalities for such a pressure-filled existence. In 1948 Roy Campanella and Don Newcombe joined Robinson on the Dodgers team, and the ageless wonder, Satchel Paige, joined the Indians. Robinson, it must be remembered, had attended college, like Paul Robeson, was a star football back, track and field performer, and basketball player at UCLA, and was used to competing with and against whites. Not every black ballplayer in the Negro leagues was, by any means, and he seemed to have sensed this difference during his one-year tour of duty with the Kansas City Monarchs. But there is no denying that Robinson was the first to attract all of the attention, and that he bore the brunt of the burden of integration. Even by 1948 integration was still an experiment in baseball—most owners were not sold on it, and there was no indication that it was necessarily here to stay. So there is no question that Robinson was exceptional as an athlete. Indeed, he was an athlete who was not merely or only an athlete for the public. He was an athlete who carried with him the meaning of his country, the belief in the virtues of its democratic values, on his back.

By 1950 Robinson was seen as heroic by most of the mainstream popular culture in America. As an example of his pop-culture presence, he was the subject of a biographical Hollywood film *The Jackie Robinson Story* in which he played himself. The intensity of his impact cannot be overestimated. He emerged as a star player in America's most popular sport at the time television became a technological force in American society. Televised baseball games spread Robinson's fame even more rapidly and thoroughly. Robinson was the first black star of the television age of popular culture. He was the subject of six late 1940s comic books released by Fawcett, a major comic book publisher of the period, in which Robinson was the Jack Armstrong-like hero, playing baseball and keeping boys on the straight and narrow. Comic books were, far and away, the most popular art form among children and adolescents in the United States, and the industry reached the height of its circulation between 1950 and 1953, the years of the Korean War, America's first armed conflict with communist countries, before protests led to a self-imposed censorship code. Comics were to continue to enjoy good sales among children after the imposition of the code, but they were never to reach the level of popularity they enjoyed in the early 1950s.[35] Other black ballplayers of the period also had comics issued: Larry Doby, Roy Campanella, Don Newcombe, and Willie Mays, an indication that these players had become, in significant measure, crossover stars, as there is no evidence that these comics were limited to the African American market. But Robinson was the only black player to have six issues, a series. Indeed, only a few white ballplayers had that many comics issued under their names, so Robinson's HUAC testimony in 1949 was a significant occurrence. After all, no one remembers the others who testified during the investigation of black loyalty. Despite the fact that the established black leadership, from Mary McLeod Bethune to Walter White, issued statements condemning Robeson, the matter came down to Robinson versus Robeson. And it must not be forgotten that Robeson, by virtue of his singing, film acting, and athletic career, was, in part, a creation of popular culture, as was Robinson, so the confrontation marked an important "first" in American race politics.[36]

Robinson's job in testifying before the HUAC was what others such as Lester Granger, the executive director of the National Urban League, and Charles S. Johnson, president of Fisk University, had done to reassure the country that blacks were loyal, that they would not "sell out" to communism, or allow themselves to be tainted by it. Robinson was to reassure the nation that blacks would, if the United States were attacked by the Soviet Union (or presumably any other enemy), fight in its support. This was certainly strange for a number of reasons, some of them not lost on Robinson at the time. In Carl

Rowan's biography of Robinson, *Wait Till Next Year*, Robinson is quoted as saying:

> I could not help but sense the irony of the fact that I, a Negro once court-martialed for opposing Army Jim Crow, should now be asked to pledge the Negro's loyalty to the Army, to the nation's military ventures. Yet life is full of ironies.

> Against the facts, Robeson's Paris remarks seemed silly to me. Even in those days of legalized peonage, when my mother was battling for a minimum standard of decency on that plantation in Georgia, Negroes had stormed the hills of San Juan with Teddy Roosevelt, for whom I was named [Robinson's middle name was Roosevelt]. . . . And in the Second World War, even in the face of insults, attacks on soldiers in their homeland, and work-horse duties in the farthest corners of the globe, the Negro had fought some, though not always with his heart in it; had sung some, even if the song was the "Bug-out Boogie," dedicated to Negroes who ran cowardly because someone had convinced them that Negroes were supposed to be cowards; still the Negro was there, as an American.

> But what about Robeson? With what was I to take issue specifically? Had Robeson betrayed me? The *Negro*? The *nation*? The *cause of freedom*? How much justification was there in the things that Robeson had said in Paris and elsewhere?
>
> Rae [Robinson's wife, Rachel] and I remembered how, as children, we had thrilled to Robeson's success, had hummed the tunes made famous by his booming bass-baritone voice.[37]

Robinson was the leading vote-getter in the fan balloting for the 1949 all-star game. If that was not, for the mainstream liberals and for the conservatives, proof that democracy worked for the Negro as well, that success could trump race, that heroism on the ball field could erase racism, then what could be? Another irony in this is that in 1943 Robeson had met with Baseball Commissioner Judge Kennesaw Mountain Landis and the major league owners to argue for the integration of the game.[38] The leftists and communists were the ones who pushed hardest for the integration of baseball, although mainstream liberals, such as the committee that produced *To Secure These Rights*, pushed for it as well.[39] Now Robinson was expected to denounce the very political impulse among blacks that insisted on social and political change in an uncompromising voice, to endorse the idea that the American Creed, Gunnar Myrdal's term from his landmark 1944 study, *An American Dilemma*, had, through its own self-awareness and self-corrective reflex, come to right its own problems. It was odd that Robinson's black heroism had wrought only the opportunity for him to ensure the white power structure that blacks were loyal to that same power structure. (It must be acknowledged, however, that some of the mail that Robinson received warning him not to testify and accusing him of being a race traitor if he did so was an organized attempt by communists to scare him.[40]) As Robinson put it years later, "Now a white man from Georgia was asking *me*, a 'refugee' from Georgia, to denounce Robeson."[41] Robinson was clearly torn: as he stated in his autobiography *I Never Had It Made:* "I was impressed by the fact that a Congressional committee had asked for my views." But he also wrote: "I didn't want to fall prey to the white man's game and allow myself to be pitted against another black man."[42] When Robinson explained the situation to Rickey, Rickey insisted that he testify. Rickey, highly religious, staunchly anti-communist, and an ardent believer in the American Creed, thought it was an honor.[43] Robinson was hardly in a position to refuse either the HUAC or Rickey. As Robinson put it to Roger Kahn years later, "Hell, [Rachel and I] weren't idiots. But Mr. Rickey *demanded* that I go. At that point in my life, if Mr. Rickey had told me to jump off the Brooklyn Bridge, I would have said, 'Head first or feet first?'"[44]

At first Rickey tried to write a statement for Robinson but gave up as Robinson seemed uncomfortable with what Rickey wrote and as it dawned on Rickey that perhaps he really could not speak very well for a black man expressing his experiences as a black man. Lester Granger, of the Urban League, is ultimately credited with writing the statement that Robinson delivered before the HUAC, although Alvin Stokes[45] also takes some credit and probably Rachel, Robinson's wife and stalwart companion, contributed as well. Granger is probably the most interesting figure and certainly shaped the statement more than anyone else. He had been among the black leaders invited in March 1948 to the White House to discuss the desegregation of the military. Granger had written an assessment of race relations in the navy for Secretary of the Navy James Forrestal, conducting his investigation between March and November 1945.[46] Granger, at the time of Rob-

inson's testimony, was serving on the Fahy Committee, the group Truman impaneled to oversee
the desegregation of the armed forces after he issued Executive Order 9981. The Fahy Committee
existed from January 1949 to July 1950, one month
after the start of the Korean War, our nation's first
war fought largely with integrated fighting troops
and where black men were given equal opportunity
to be on the front lines. So Granger is an important
figure in all of this, a black liberal with the ear of
the president and the head of an important mainstream civil rights organization and preoccupied
with the integration of the armed forces. Indeed,
Granger probably knew more about the status of
blacks in the armed forces than most other black
leaders. In the end this is reflected in Robinson's
statement: direct mention of the integration of the
military, granting equal opportunity to all, alluded
to when Robinson speaks about the limited number of blacks in the major leagues, and so forth.
But the statement reassures the nation that blacks
are loyal and will fight for their country as they
fight against discrimination. In that sense, Robinson's statement, in part, is nothing more than a
restatement of the double-V campaign of the liberal black leadership during World War II: victory

for democracy in the war against fascism overseas and victory for democracy at home in the battle against racism. What Robinson ultimately delivered was not so much a put-down or a refutation of Robeson directly, although he does mention that Negroes are not inclined to throw away what they have invested in their country's welfare "because of a siren song sung in bass," as the speech was an endorsement, an important one considering Robinson's position in American society at the time, of mainstream, anti-communist, civil rights liberalism, of the self-correcting possibilities inherent in the American Creed of equality and fairness. Robinson's job, in appearing in front of the HUAC, was basically to implicitly endorse *To Secure These Rights*, which is what he did.

And Robinson implicitly supported the integration of the military. After all, Lieutenant Jack Roosevelt Robinson had been court-martialed at Fort Hood, Texas, because on July 6, 1944, he refused to go to the back of an army bus after being ordered to do so by the driver. When Robinson stood up for himself against a white superior officer who met him when he was placed under the arrest, Robinson was charged with insubordination, a serious charge. With the help of other black officers who wrote letters to the *Pittsburgh Courier* and the *Chicago Defender*, the case became something of a hot potato. The case came to trial on August 2, 1944, and Robinson beat the charges.[47] So Robinson already had a reputation in the black community as someone who had stood up against institutionalized racism, as he had become a symbol against it in major league baseball. What better black person was there to validate the liberal ideology of integration and equality than Robinson and have it carry some conviction with both blacks and whites?

Robinson said, in part, in his testimony before the HUAC:

I don't pretend to be any expert on communism or any other political "ism". . . . But put me down as an expert on being a colored American, with thirty years' experience. And just like any other colored person with sense enough to look around him and understand what he sees, I know that life in these United States can be mighty tough for people who are a little different from the majority—in their skin color or the way they worship their God, or the way they spell their names.

I'm not fooled because I've had a chance open to very few Negro Americans. It's true that I've been the laboratory specimen in a great change in organized baseball. I'm proud that I've made good on my assignment to the point where other colored players will find it easier to enter the game and go to the top. But I'm very well aware that even this limited job isn't finished yet. There are only three major league clubs with only seven colored players signed up, out of close to four hundred major league players on sixteen clubs . . .

The white public should start appreciating that every single Negro worth his salt resents slurs and discrimination. That has absolutely nothing to do with what Communists may or may not be trying to do.

And white people must realize that the more a Negro hates communism because it opposes democracy, the more he is going to hate any other influence that kills off democracy in this country—racial discrimination in the army, segregation on trains and buses, job discrimination because of religious beliefs.

If a Communist denounces injustice in the American courts, or police brutality, or lynching, when it happens, that doesn't change the truth of his charges. Just because Communists kick up a big fuss over racial discrimination when it suits their purpose, a lot of people try to pretend that the whole issue is a creation of Communist imaginations. . . . Negroes were stirred up long before there was a Communist party, and they'll stay stirred up long after the party has disappeared—unless Jim Crow had disappeared by then as well.

I understand that there are some few Negroes who are members of the Communist party, and in event of war with Russia they would probably act just as any other Communists would. So would members of other minority and majority groups. . . . Most Negroes—and Italians and Irish and Jews and Swedes and Slavs and other Americans—would act just as all these groups did in the last war. They'd do their best to help their country stay out of war; if unsuccessful, they'd do their best to help their country win the war—against Russia or any other enemy that threatened us. . . .

What I'm trying to get across is that the American public is off on the wrong foot when it begins to think of radicalism in terms of any special minority group. It is thinking of this sort that gets people scared because one Negro, speaking to a Communist group in Paris, threatens an organized boycott by 15 million members of his race. . . .

I am a religious man. Therefore, I cherish America, where I am free to worship as I please, a privilege which some countries do not give. And I suspect that 999 out of almost any 1,000 colored Americans you meet will tell you the same thing.

But that doesn't mean that we're going to stop fighting race discrimination in this country until we've got it licked. It means that we're going to fight it all the harder because our stake in the future is so big. We can win our fight without the Communists and we don't want their help.[48]

Robinson received ecstatic applause in the committee room. The speech was praised in the white press and generally was well received in the black press, but there was more disappointment and skepticism expressed about it among African Americans. Some were even angry, for many blacks felt Robeson to be courageous and outspoken in speaking the truth. After all, from a black perspective, Robeson must be speaking the truth; otherwise, he would not be losing concert bookings and be savagely disparaged by the white press and white political leaders. This is how the oppressed judge who speaks the truth on their behalf, and it is certainly sensible enough if it avoids endorsing demagoguery. Robinson's statement is noted for its restraint. He does acknowledge in his speech that he found Robeson's statement "silly, if Mr. Robeson actually made it," an allusion to the fact that Robeson had been in touch with Robinson before he had made his appearance before the HUAC and had told him that his remarks had been distorted by the press. Robinson reminds the HUAC and the nation that he is a religious man, as are the vast majority of black people, meaning that they are not susceptible to godless communism. (This is an old trope about the character of blacks, going back as far as Booker T. Washington in his attempts to sell blacks to the white power structure as anti-subversive by nature.) But Robinson also makes it clear that blacks are fighting and will continue to fight to defeat Jim Crow. Further, he argues that his success does not mean that blacks have it made or that the fight, even in major league baseball, is over. He simply wishes to reiterate that blacks could be loyal Americans and still battle to become full and equal citizens in the realm, that one did not preclude the other— the standard integrationist position of the 1950s (nonradical dissent was manly and part of the American tradition, an expression of the American Creed), forcefully and lyrically articulated a few years later by Ralph Ellison in *Invisible Man*, which suggested, in the end, a multicultural America, and a few years after that by James Baldwin, in *Notes of a Native Son*, both book and essay, where the young Negro son refutes the isolation and bitterness of his hate-filled father. And there was more than a touch of the son refuting the bitterness of a radical father figure in Robinson's testimony.

But to refute all traces of radicalism in black protest, to deny any connection between the African American struggle and a larger radical critique of America, seems not just inaccurate historically and politically but somehow seems to diminish the very nature of that protest in the challenge that it posed to American life and culture. That was dangerously naïve. And Robinson became aware of how naïve he was when Robeson concertgoers were attacked a few weeks later at Peekskill in New York's Westchester County. An anti-Robeson mob smashed the stage where Robeson was to perform, set fire to the seats, "and put a dozen Robeson supporters in the hospital."[49]

On June 25, 1950, the Korean War erupted when communist North Korea invaded U.S.-supported

South Korea. In a way Robinson was something like the poster child for that war inasmuch as it dealt with the integration of the military. Robinson had shown that integration could work in American professional life, but at the cost of the denigration and undoing of any structures of black institutional life, such as they were, as segregated black life in America was meant to be institutionally deprived. When major league baseball—and the minor league structure that supplemented it—was called "organized baseball," it was implied that everything else, particularly the Negro leagues, was "unorganized" or "disorganized." This became a stigma in African American cultural and institutional life. Integrated major league baseball meant the demise of the Negro leagues, which was not, by any means, a bad thing, as the Negro leagues should never have been made by political circumstances to exist to begin with. But the fact of its clearly imperfect existence was something of a strenuous accomplishment. During the war, the integration of the armed forces was symbolically enacted through the demise of the 24th Infantry Regiment, one of the last all-black units in the army. The 24th was one of the first units to go to Korea and, like the others, black and white, it was ill prepared for battle and often did not perform well. Men ran from battle, and the

song "Bug-out Boogie," which Robinson mentioned in his 1949 testimony, became associated
with the 24th. Indeed, people commonly thought
that the 24th made up the song, although it clearly
existed before the Korean War, as Robinson's testimony made clear. Also, "bugging out" was a term
used by both blacks and whites in the military.
Whites ran as much if not more than blacks in the
opening weeks of the Korean War. It was the 24th
that was the subject of news articles, and it was the
24th that produced a number of courts-martial, as
black soldiers were more harshly treated than whites
for the same infractions. So flagrant were these un-
fair courts-martial that the NAACP in January 1951
sent Thurgood Marshall to Japan and Korea to investigate. The most famous court-martial out of the
24th was that of Lieutenant Leon Gilbert who, on
July 30, 1950, refused a direct order from a superior to
take his men on what he felt was a suicide mission.
He was at first condemned to death, but the sentence was later commuted, in part because of the
outcry of the black press about Gilbert's situation,
to twenty years of hard labor. The inefficiency and
ineffectiveness of all-black units, perceived and
real, brought about the integration of the army, but
the redemption of the reputation of black fighting

men was brought about only at the expense of their reputation as black fighting men who fought as blacks.[50] The integration of the army was good for both black soldiers and for the army as a whole. However, not only was the process something of an ordeal, but it was effected at a cost to the very men it benefited. So when the outsider becomes something of an insider, does he or she subvert the establishment or simply symbolize its greatness by being absorbed by it? By what do we measure the meaning of accommodation and resistance, acceptance and subversion? Are these very binary terms meant to describe the outsider going inside as a sign of how we so crudely simplify human motivation, ambition, and accomplishment to fit a narrow moral vision of guilt and redemption in our own minds? And who is to claim for the outsider which mode is the more heroic? Should he, finally, be Samson or Joseph?

Robinson had become a fairly unpopular player in the 1950s; sportswriters wrote a great deal more negatively about him. They felt he was overly sensitive and that he argued too much, behaving much like the persecuted minority once he was on the inside: he could only complain about what was not there and what had not been done. Of course, there were white players like this about whom far less complaints were raised. But Robinson was the cultural paradigm of the age. Films about integration in the late 1940s through the 1950s tended to be versions of the Jackie Robinson story, from *Home of the Brave*, with James Edwards as a black soldier in an all-white unit, to *No Way Out*, with Sidney Poitier as a black doctor at a white hospital, from *Red Ball Express*, about an integrated support unit during World War II learning to work together under a white officer, to *Pork Chop Hill*, in part about a disgruntled black soldier, Woody Strode, who shirks his duty at first but comes around in the end, to *All the Young Men*, with Sidney Poitier as a sergeant put in charge of an all-white unit.[51] (Jackie Robinson as the first black manager, something that was on the minds of some of the sporting public at the time. Branch Rickey wrote, "Give him complete control of emotion and I know of no one better qualified for major league management."[52]) Most of these films, unsurprisingly, were about the military, probably because the military offered the closest analogy to the kind of organizational setup one finds with high-performance sports teams and because the integration of the military was the major *and* most successful institutional change regarding race (and males) in the life of the United States during the cold war, except for American professional and amateur sports. Jackie Robinson, alas, was our constrained hero in the age of the cold war, the charismatic prince of an old-style liberalism that believed in the individual more than it believed in the viability of group identities, that believed in merit more than in reparations, and that believed more in the legitimacy of American institutions and their fundamental fairness than in a racial nihilism that thought the plague of white supremacy could not be cured except by political amputation. But he was also the great black representative man, who knew more tellingly than anyone else, as a tormented lion in his brief, tough middle age, that no great black athlete is only an athlete.

2

Curt Flood, Gratitude, and the Image of Baseball

. . . they go by the creed "keep them grateful."
—College defensive back Bobby Smith on
why he was not drafted by an NFL or
AFL team in 1968 after he had become a
spokesman for militant African American
athletes on campus

WHEN ST. LOUIS CARDINALS center fielder
Curt Flood refused to submit to being traded to the
Philadelphia Phillies in October 1969, after twelve
years of service with the Cardinals as one of their
best players and fourteen years of service overall in
professional baseball, he helped redefine how athletes, particularly black athletes, were seen by the
public and the press in the United States.

The trade itself had racial and political over-
tones: true, the Cardinals probably wanted a power

hitter for the middle of their lineup, and Dick Allen, also called Richie, the major player they received from Philadelphia in the trade for Flood, was one of the best power hitters in the game, having hit forty homers once and over thirty homers twice during his six years with the Phillies as a regular starting player. And it was also probably true that the Phillies were seeking both better defense and more speed, and Flood was one of the speediest and one of the best defensive outfielders in the game, although he was more than three years older than Allen and could not match his overall run production. Most important, however, was that both men were black and both were causing, from management's point of view, problems with their teams; teams often decide, depending on the particular skills a player may possess, to swap problems. Indeed, it was almost a certainty that if a team wanted to trade a black "problem" player in 1969, considering the reality of quotas for black players on most professional sports teams at that time, then it was going to have to take a black "problem" player in return. In other words Allen and Flood were traded for each other, aside from their skills and the particular needs their respective teams had, because, as they were both "problem" players, they likely could not have been traded for anyone else. The Cardinals had won back-to-back National League pennants in 1967 and 1968 but were a dispirited team in 1969, finishing fourth in the National League Eastern Division, thirteen games out of first place. Flood blamed the team's dismal performance on two events: a speech given to the team by owner and beer magnate August A. Busch Jr. during spring training on March 22, 1969, and on trading, a few days later, Orlando Cepeda, known among his teammates as Cha-Cha, the team's popular first baseman to Atlanta in exchange for Joe Torre. Busch's speech was largely a diatribe in defense of baseball owners: how costly it was to field a major league team, how much work was involved in getting people to come out to the games, and how much owners did to elevate the image and status of the ballplayer:

> It used to be that some parents looked down their noses at the thought of their sons going into professional baseball.
>
> Today, that's all changed. Making the grade in the major leagues is just about the most productive thing that could happen to a young man.
>
> In addition to being well paid during his baseball days, there are even greater opportuni-

ties for a player to make lasting and profitable business connections, mostly because they played major league baseball.

Many of you have already done that. Stan Musial, Lou Brock, Curt Flood, Tim McCarver, Roger Maris, and many others are already in that category. And you know it.

True, you deserve to be well paid in accordance with your playing ability. But I must call your attention to the fact of life that you take few, if any, of the great risks involved.[1]

Busch concluded his speech by deploring all of the recent talk in the off-season about the players' pension fund and the possibility of a strike, saying that such talk did not go over well with the fans. "They are the ones who make you popular. They are the ones who make your salary and pension possible."[2] In effect Busch seemed to be berating his players for being ungrateful, a charge that was to be made in several quarters about ballplayers generally during this period as they became more union conscious and more militant in their demands with the owners, and a charge that was being made against black athletes during this period as they had become more self-consciously racial and political. Busch made his speech only a few months after the 1968 Olympic Games in Mexico City, where sprinters Tommie Smith and John Carlos made clenched-fist "black power" salutes during their medal-awarding ceremony. Boxer Muhammad Ali was already famous around the world for his stance against the draft and the Vietnam War and had been banned from boxing. The racial integration of high-performance athletics in the United States was still very much a work in progress at this time, and the latest generation of black athletes seemed, like the black population in general, more angry about the present than grateful about how much of an improvement the present was over the past.

Flood, a black player on a team with other star blacks—Lou Brock and Bob Gibson, both Hall of Fame players now—and a huge black Latino star, Orlando Cepeda, who was there during several of the Cardinals glory years and who is now also in the Hall of Fame—described his response to Busch's speech: "During 1969, I protested more vigorously than usual, and even broke into print a few times. This did not endear me to management. Especially not at $90,000 a year."[3] He felt, by the end of 1969, that he would be traded because he was known as a troublemaker and because he made so much money.

He called himself the highest-paid singles hitter in the game at that time. Flood was on a successful team that had won two World Series during his tenure, and he had several overachieving black teammates. Flood had an artistic bent and ran a portrait painting and photography business as a sideline to his baseball career. He also was something of a free spirit, visiting places such as Copenhagen and imbibing a bit in a black male bohemian lifestyle so richly satirized in Cecil Brown's brilliant 1969 comic novel *The Life and Loves of Mr. Jiveass Nigger.*

Dick (Richie) Allen's situation was a little different. Despite such black and Latino players as Ruben Amaro, Tony Taylor, Tony Gonzalez, Wes Covington, Ted Savage, and Johnny Briggs, Allen was the first true black superstar to play in Philadelphia. No Hall of Fame players of color were in his cohort on that team. In this sense he operated under even more pressure and more scrutiny than Flood as the big black star. Allen was Rookie of the Year in 1964, when the Phillies nearly won the National League pennant. It was the same year the city experienced a major race riot in the North Philadelphia ghetto area, where Connie Mack Stadium, where the Phillies played, was located. A group of merchants sponsored a "Richie Allen Night" in September

1964, during the midst of the team's infamous collapse that cost them the pennant, an unusual honor for a rookie player, fueling the idea that Allen was being given special treatment, and all the more so, perhaps, because of the riot. Despite Allen's offensive heroics, the team never won a pennant in the 1960s. Allen was a much misunderstood man; he seemed to like horses and cars better than people, and many thought he squandered his enormous talent. He would sometimes disappear for several days during the season, prompting many to think him lazy and uncommitted. He got into a highly publicized fight in 1965 with white infielder Frank Thomas, during which Thomas hit Allen with a bat after Allen slugged him for using a racial slur, which resulted in Thomas being waived and Allen being booed by Philadelphia crowds. The white public and some white sportswriters began to think that there were separate rules for Allen, that he was indulged not only because he was a star but because he was black. (For much of the white public, the age of black militancy had produced the petulant black athlete, befuddled by the complex industry in which his or her own talent was rewarded and exploited, and bemused by the fact that he or she existed largely as a product of white patronage or white goodwill.) It became a popular notion that the Phillies operated under two realities: one for Allen, and one for the other twenty-four men on the team. "One of Richie's biggest supporters," wrote black sportswriter Bill Nunn Jr. in 1968, "is team owner Bob Carpenter. The two get along well. They seldom have serious contract difficulties. Yet if you listen to the Philly press it comes out that Richie is teacher's pet and is coddled by the boss."[4] When manager Gene Mauch was fired in June 1968, it was commonly believed that Allen went to Carpenter with a "Mauch or Me" ultimatum and got his way.[5] He was the most disliked player on the team by the Philadelphia public, particularly whites, in a city with a considerable white ethnic population, especially blue-collar Italians and Irish Catholics. Allen nearly ended his career in August 1967 when he accidentally cut the tendons in his hand when he pushed his hand through his car's headlight when trying to move the vehicle after it had stalled in the rain. Allen never fully recovered from his hand injury, but he played for ten more years as a highly productive player. By 1968, because of the constant booing, the throwing of objects (Allen took to wearing his batting helmet in the field and was nicknamed "Crash," as in crash helmet), and bad press, Allen desperately wanted to be traded. Both Allen and Flood were very different black men with different abilities and different playing experiences; Flood did not want to be traded from St. Louis, and Allen wanted to get out of Philadelphia in any way he could. Yet both men were alike in interesting ways—they were both heavy smokers and drinkers, but neither let these habits affect their performance on the field, although Allen drank during games;[6] both were incredibly tense men and high strung, possessing habits and personalities that symbolized and reflected the highly stressful world of the pressurized performance of the professional athlete, probably a tad more pressurized for the black professional athlete.[7] Both, by the end of their 1960s tenures with their respective teams, were considered troublemakers, albeit of very different sorts. One was artistic, outspoken, and concerned about social justice issues; the other was moody, uncommunicative, isolated, and almost trapped within his own psyche. Rejecting the idea of representing anything to anyone, and especially the bearing of the Joe Louis/Jackie Robinson exemplar as a black athlete, Allen once said, speaking about himself: "You're supposed to be an example. Why do I have be an example for your kid? You be an example for your own kid."[8] Both were condemned by many because they no longer seemed to appreciate what baseball had done *for* them. They both expressed something, one more articulately than the other, but each in his own passionate way, that troubled the public and press deeply—a profound concern about what baseball had done *to* them. Interestingly, at the time of the Flood controversy, Allen thought that Flood would play for the Phillies in 1970 because of the money.[9] Yet Allen's complaint about being in Philadelphia echoed Flood's complaint about the response to his lawsuit and the complaint of successful black athletes generally during this period: "But in Philadelphia, their attitude was that I should be *grateful* just to be allowed on the field. The sportswriters there would make things worse by comparing my salary to other players in the league that had been around longer."[10] But whether Flood decided to play was immaterial to Allen; he was never going to return to Philadelphia.[11]

What I wish to examine in this chapter is not how or why Flood's legal challenge to this trade precipitated the rush of events, if indeed it did, that produced modified free agency for baseball players in the mid-1970s with the Messersmith-McNally labor relations settlement that so changed the salary structure of the sport, by so radically changing the bargaining position of veteran players. I leave that to others who are far more knowledgeable about the complex issues involved in the labor-management relationship of major league baseball. What I am more interested in is how African Americans began to perceive sports quite differently in the 1960s, sensing in some way that sports simply replicated their relatively powerless political and social position in the larger society; that participating in sports, even on a highly successful level, did not liberate either the individual athlete or his group in any significant way; that sports were, in the main, dehumanizing; and how this new perception was related to how some members of the press responded to a particular aspect of the Flood challenge, the idea that Flood was a slave because of the conditions under which he played under baseball's reserve clause, placing that response within the historical, cultural, and political context of the moment of the late 1960s and the growing sense among the press, the public, and the baseball owners that baseball players generally were ungrateful for their good fortune, and the same growing sense in some of the white press, white management, and among the white public that black athletes were generally ungrateful for what sports had done for African Americans. I am reminded that there was a sense in the late 1960s, a very turbulent time in American social history, among many whites that blacks were, on the whole, ungrateful for the changes that had been made on their behalf as a result of the civil rights movement. It was commonplace to hear cries among whites of "What do blacks want?" or "What more do they want?" With the civil rights agitation came, of course, a white reaction or, as it was called in the 1960s, a white backlash against further reform or, as some whites saw it, the further granting of concessions, as whites feared that blacks were moving from being a stigmatized caste to becoming a specially privileged group of sentimentalized victims. And, naturally, there was nostalgia among many for the old days when blacks "knew their place." Flood exacerbated this mood among many whites when he sued baseball in 1970 but particularly because he sued not only on the grounds that baseball's reserve clause, which prevented him from contesting the trade, was not only a violation of federal antitrust law but also was a violation of the Thirteenth Amendment that outlawed involuntary servitude. The fact that Flood was black intensified the significance of this particular attack against baseball's reserve clause; the fact that the black athlete was becoming more and more politicized in the 1960s and that some saw performing sports as a form of slavery made this attack all the more a reflection of the great racial divide that afflicted the country. Many whites and even some blacks asked: "How can they hate performing sports or find them demeaning when sports have been so good to the Negro?"

THE SLAVERY METAPHOR AND THE MEANING OF THE AFRICAN AMERICAN PRESENCE IN SPORTS

Throughout his famous 1969 book, *The Revolt of the Black Athlete*, Harry Edwards made a number of references to slavery, often comparing the modern-day black athlete to a slave or the practices of modern-day, high-performance athletics to slavery. For instance he called college recruitment "the modern-day equivalent of the slave trade";[12] he distinguished the white athlete from the black athlete who is "reduced to a slave-with-pay status";[13] and he stated a bit later that "[like] the black slave who sang songs and hummed tunes as he toiled in the fields, the black professional athlete has, too, traditionally accommodated himself to the discrimination and racism he has encountered in professional sports. And, as was the case with the black slave, so successful has his masquerade been that many naive, ignorant, or openly racist whites actually believed that the black professional athlete was in fact not humiliated or enraged by the treatment he received."[14] Edwards later wrote, "Taking a page from the slave's book on survival tactics, the black pro learned to turn the other cheek when his impulse was to kill, to smile when his impulse was to curse."[15] In keeping with the motif of the black athlete as a kind of slave, Edwards also made the point several times that black athletes were not considered human beings in the sports industry but a form of chattel. "The black athlete in professional athletics is regarded by most of his white comrades and owners as a machine—a machine to be used as white men see fit and then discarded after youth has gone or injury has reduced it to the point where cost has surpassed production. Then the 'machine' is simply traded in for a newer model."[16] Edwards stated earlier: "Like a piece of equipment, the black athlete is used."[17] Elsewhere he wrote this about athletes generally: "All professional athletes—black and white—are officially and formally classified as property."[18]

Ex-American League baseball star Larry Doby, who entered major league baseball only one month after Jackie Robinson in 1947, said much the same in a 1968 issue of *Sports Illustrated*: "Black athletes are cattle. They're raised, fed, sold, and killed."[19] It did not surprise people that Edwards would say the sort of things that he was saying, but it surprised a good many people at the time to hear Doby say that.

Several times during his exile from boxing between 1967 and 1970, Muhammad Ali was to make the same comparison of the black athlete to the slave. In the May 1970 issue of *Esquire*, Ali said, "Fighters are just brutes that come to entertain the rich white people. Beat up on each other and break each other's noses, and bleed, and show off like two little monkeys for the crowd, killing each other for the crowd. *And half of the crowd is white.* We just like two slaves in the ring. The master gets two of us big old black slaves and let us fight it out while they bet. 'My slave can whup your slave.' That's what I see when I see two black people fighting." Later in the same article Ali talks about his nemesis, Joe Frazier: "All his Cloverlay, Inc., stockholders who own him are gathered around him, acting like he's their racehorse. That's just the way my white managers were: investing in me, buying and selling stock in me, getting on trains for the big fights, like they were going to some kind of slave festival, to watch their slaves perform."[20] He repeated himself nearly verbatim in an interview published a month later in *The Black Scholar*: "We're slaves in that ring. The masters get two of us big ones and let us fight it out while they bet. 'My slave can beat your slave.'"[21] Ali made these remarks the same year Flood filed suit against baseball's reserve clause. Ali certainly had not been influenced by Flood's stance against the reserve clause as constituting a form of slavery in formulating his thinking. He had been thinking about boxing in this way probably since he officially became a member of the Nation of Islam in 1964.[22] Almost certainly he had heard ideas of this sort as early as 1964, when he first fought Sonny Liston for the title and was good friends with Malcolm X, who held such beliefs himself. The Nation of Islam disparaged sports and blacks in popular culture, generally. Flood, though, had been almost certainly influenced by Ali's stance against the Vietnam War. But the larger issue here, I think, is that black athletic performance as a form of slavery, that the black athlete is seen as a thing, not a person, had become a kind of zeitgeist. Blacks had offered opinions like this before, for instance, abolitionist Frederick Douglass when he talked about sporting activities on the plantation in his autobiographies, and Marxist writer Richard Wright when he covered Joe Louis's fights in the 1930s.[23] But generally blacks saw sports as an arena where they could compete with whites head-to-head on the basis of something as close as humanly possible to objective merit. Indeed, the idea of sports as the great meritocracy made the ideology of sports as a component of American liberalism very appealing to many blacks. But in the 1960s this idea of blacks in sports as a subtle form of degradation or dehumanization had become nearly commonplace. It was an indication of how much liberalism was in a state of crisis, of how much American institutions were afflicted by a crisis of legitimation, because race challenged the prevailing notion of how institutions worked even after, and especially after, blacks were included in these institutions as signs of good business and fair democratic practice. Liberalism did not seem to have changed the dynamics of paternalism but, rather, at least from the perspective of blacks, to have absorbed them. And nothing seemed more paternalistic than sports, with its roots partly in nineteenth-century American slavery and in the nineteenth-century American capitalism of monopoly and ownership domination.[24]

The comparison of the high-performance athlete to a slave certainly was made before Flood's case. In the first of his noted five-part series on the black athlete, written for *Sports Illustrated* in 1968, Jack Olsen quoted a Big Ten basketball coach as saying: "'Things are now getting to the point where all a coach has to do is go out and pick up four or five good Negro players and let things take their natural course. In order to succeed—which means to win—coaches are being forced to resort to what I would bluntly call nothing else but the slave trade.'"[25] *Ebony* magazine's April 1964 photo-editorial was entitled "Needed—An Abe Lincoln of Baseball." It dealt with the unfairness of professional baseball's reserve clause, and this was six years before Flood sued baseball:

> When Abraham Lincoln inked his angular letters at the bottom of the Emancipation Proclamation in 1863, there were many who thought this marked the end of slavery. . . . To all intents and purposes, it freed the slave in the United States

for all times. But what Abe, a true lover of sports (he was a wrestler of considerable skill), didn't know was that in the United States under the guise of a great national pastime, a form of semi-slavery would grow and flourish, seemingly with the whole-hearted approval of the public and the government. If anyone would tell Willie [Mays] that he was "slave labor," the highest paid player in baseball (he is said to be the man earning around $110,000) would probably laugh himself silly. But what would his answer be if you asked him why he didn't check with the Yankees of the American League to see if maybe they wouldn't pay him $125,000 a year for his services?[26]

The *Ebony* editorial, after explaining how the re-serve clause made it impossible for Mays to negotiate with another team for a higher salary, as he was the property of his club for life or to the club to which his club may choose to trade or sell him, then discussed the fate of two white ballplayers: Yankee pitcher Jim Bouton, who was forced to sign for less than he wanted and far less than his market value after he had won twenty-one games the previous year, simply because the club gave him a take-it-or-leave-it offer, which the reserve clause gave them the power to do; and Chicago White Sox relief pitcher Jim Brosnan, who was released because he wrote articles during the baseball season. The editorial expressed concern that the major league clubs may have the power, through the reserve clause, to restrict players in other ways: "There might be a restriction on speaking at Urban League and NAACP rallies. Come to think of it, major league ballplayers have not been very evident in the forefront of equal rights demonstrations." The article, after mentioning that major league baseball owners had exercised the right to determine who could play, not on the basis of talent but skin color, concluded: "As a general rule, we do not object to baseball's privileges. But when these privileges deprive a man of his right to write for magazines, keep a man from joining in a fight for freedom, or limit his earning ability just because he must play for a certain team, we wonder."[27] What is striking here is that a middle-of-the-road black magazine, fixated with the notion of bourgeois accomplishment, which made a fetish of black material success and social status, should make an issue of baseball's reserve clause and question the political commitment and economic remuneration of black baseball stars, among the most revered black figures of popular culture in the

1960s,[28] especially at a time when it was not a pressing public or pressing black issue. *Ebony's* concern about how much the reserve clause stifled the black baseball player's political expression was partly substantiated in 1968 when an anonymous black baseball star said: "'Baseball players can't stick their noses out and say things about racial injustice. . . . We can't negotiate for ourselves because of the reserve clause. There are no other leagues. Either you sign with your team or you don't play baseball."[29]

Jack Olsen's series of articles on the black athlete in America that appeared in *Sports Illustrated* in the summer of 1968 made clear that black athletes, as a group, were "dissatisfied, disgruntled, and disillusioned." Tired of a quota system that kept the number of black professional and college athletes at a certain number, cynical about the phenomenon of stacking that kept blacks from playing certain "leadership" positions in certain sports, disillusioned by the experience of being scholar-athletes at white universities from where few graduated and most felt alienated and isolated, disenchanted with the fact that they had to outperform whites in order to remain in their chosen sport and yet had virtually no future in the sport once their playing days were over, and discouraged by the lack of opportunities for product endorsements, despite having huge seasons on the field, blacks were becoming more vocal in expressing their feelings about the shortcomings of a sports career as an entry into mainstream America. But this unhappiness, which went to the heart of the role of the intersection of athletics and race in the affirmation of the ideology of American liberalism, was not received very well by many sports fans or sportswriters, some of whom, naturally, felt threatened by such feelings on the part of blacks. "The Negro athlete who has the nerve to suggest that all is not perfect," wrote Olsen in 1968, "is branded as ungrateful, a cur that bites the hand."[30] Understanding the historical moment, it is certainly no surprise that Flood, a thoughtful man, deeply proud and sensitive, with a somewhat ironical turn of mind, would make such statements in his 1971 autobiography as "[The trade] violated the logic and integrity of my existence. I was not a consignment of goods. I was a man, the rightful proprietor of my own person and my own talents,"[31] saying this right after he had talked about the proximity of the Pruitt-Igoe housing project to the old courthouse "in which Dred Scott sued for his freedom. From the shattered windows of the worst of the slums . . . 10,000 inheritors of old Dred's disappointment are free to enjoy superb views of the arch and to draw what conclusions they will."[32] Or, "'I just won't be treated as if I were an IBM card.'"[33] Or, "'I do not feel that I am a piece of property to be bought and sold irrespective of my wishes.'"[34] Flood knew well how inextricably bound the idea of gratitude, with the paternalistic liberalism of American sports, was with the white public idea of how a black person should feel about his success. "The proprietors and publicists of baseball could be depended on to remind me of [my advancing age and eroding skill] at every turn, meanwhile reviling me in print as a destroyer, an ingrate, a fanatic, a dupe."[35] He described a piece of hate mail he received where the writer reminded him "that if it were not for the great game of baseball I would be chopping cotton or pushing a broom. And that I was a discredit to my race."[36] Flood also talked at great length about how the professional baseball industry itself, with its shills and sportswriters, fosters the attitude of gratitude by mythologizing the game, tying it vividly to the idea of the American national character and propagandizing it as a symbol of American democratic values, thus masterfully and subtly turning the public against any player who does not publicly express that he feels blessed to be playing the game. As Flood wrote: "The only approved posture is one of tail-wagging thanks for the opportunities provided by the employer. Few active players feel anything like such gratitude, and none has reason to. Baseball employment is too insecure for that. Not many players deliver their ceremonial recitations [of gratitude] without a sense of embarrassment."[37] And so Flood's challenge of baseball not only, as Flood saw it, cost him his career but cost him virtually everything. In 1978, six years after the Supreme Court ruled against Flood, despite saying in its ruling that no rational basis existed for baseball to have a reserve clause and to be exempted from anti-trust laws when every other sport had been subject to them, Richard Reeves went looking for Curt Flood. When he finally reached him, Flood said to him in heartbreaking desperation: "'Please, please don't come out here. Don't bring it all up again. Please. Do you know what I've been through? Do you know what it means to go against the grain of the country? Your neighbors hate you. Do you know what it's like to be called the little black son of a bitch who tried to destroy baseball, the American Pastime?'"[38] In retrospect it is not surprising that Flood would take the stance he did at that particular moment, when the black zeitgeist was to challenge all of the assumptions about what affirmed American liberalism, and especially to attack the legitimacy of color-blind merit, which sports had so promoted, as a mask for the maintenance of white power.[39] It is also not surprising that because he challenged baseball, a sport so deeply connected to the country's sense of itself as it would imagine itself to be, a sport, more than any other, that fosters incredible national self-deception, that because he challenged it in the way he did, that he would think that the end of his baseball career was rather a form of conspiratorial destruction. Flood's own self-mythology as activist/martyr consists of two beliefs: his challenge destroyed him, and he was destroyed because he was a *black* man who challenged an entrenched system. As baseball becomes more self-consciously multicultural (for instance, Major League Baseball invented the Civil Rights Game in 2007, first as a spring training game and then in 2009 as a regular season game, as a tribute to blacks and their struggle against racism) and develops a history to fit that ideological frame, a black person as a sacrificial lamb, in this instance, who freed the peon/players, as it were, may wind up serving many people, including the lords of baseball themselves, a great deal of public good. In the end, the Flood challenge may convince many that Larry Doby was right when he said in 1968: "Baseball has done a lot for the Negro but the Negro has done more for baseball."[40]

The Press, Curt Flood, and the Idea of Involuntary Servitude

In his discussion of the Flood case in his *Sociology of Sports* (1973), Harry Edwards quotes part of federal judge Irving Ben Cooper's decision to deny Flood's suit: "'The plaintiff's $90,000 a year salary does not support the spirit of his assertion that the reserve clause relegates him to a condition of involuntary servitude. For if it did, he would be the highest paid slave in history.'"[41] The fact that Cooper based his ruling in this way on Flood's contention that the reserve clause was a violation of the Thirteenth Amendment's anti-involuntary servitude clause (he could have simply said that the clause was not applicable because Flood was paid for his services, which precluded any sense that he was an involuntary servant in the sense that the amendment meant; it would not matter, in this understanding of the clause, how much he was being paid; slaves are not paid, period), and that Edwards, in his discussion of the case, chose to highlight it, reveals how much this case turned in the minds of many not on the more complex technical issue of anti-trust law but on the visceral issue of whether Flood was a slave in any sense of that term based on the amount of money he was paid when he last played baseball for the Cardinals. (Flood did return to baseball briefly in 1971 as an outfielder for the Washington Senators, but after a dismal start he quit baseball for good after about a month. He would have earned over $100,000 had he stayed with the team for the season, or at least beyond May 15.[42]) In a sense the Flood case was about whether paternalism, as a mythologized form of an employer's benevolence and an employee's gratitude, remained an essential component of the nation's understanding of liberalism, more than one hundred years after the end of slavery as a system built on that very idea as a democratic value. As so many found it difficult to side with Flood because of his salary (and his privileged status was doubtless intensified by his race, the fact that he was a black man making a salary that few black men at the time were eligible to make), it would seem that the powerful attack made against paternalism in Harriet Beecher Stowe's famous 1852 novel, *Uncle Tom's Cabin* (two of Tom's three masters are benevolent, are models of white paternalism, but neither protects Tom, one from selfish convenience and the other from negligence, when he is sold from family and friends), never truly seeped into the collective American consciousness. We only remember the brutal Simon Legree.

Some mainstream sportswriters supported Flood, such as Jim Murray, who in his column "Uncle Curt's Cabin" wrote, "The 'reserve clause,' to be sure, is just a fancy name for slavery. The only thing it doesn't let the owners do is flog their help."[43] Red Smith, also sympathetic to Flood, felt that the question of whether the abolition of the reserve clause would destroy baseball, the claim made by the owners at Flood's trials, was the wrong issue entirely. "First it should be agreed that ownership of people is repugnant per se and that a business which depends for its existence upon such evil isn't necessarily worth saving."[44] When the trade was first announced, Flood said that he would retire and continue to paint portraits, which he had been doing with modest success for several years before the trade. The former Cardinals general manager, Frank Lane, said, upon hearing this, "Flood will play next year . . .

unless he's better than Rembrandt." To this, Smith responded: "It was a beautiful comment, superlatively typical of the executive mind, a pluperfect example of baseball's reaction to unrest down in the slave cabins. Baseball demands incredulously, 'You mean that at these prices, they want human rights, too?'"[45]

The black press, although some thought Flood made a bad decision to challenge the reserve clause, was generally sympathetic and supportive. Bill Nunn Jr. of *The Pittsburgh Courier* pointed out the hypocrisy in how baseball executives viewed Flood and how they viewed pitcher Denny McLain (who won thirty-one games for the Detroit Tigers in 1968) who was found to have a financial interest in a bookmaking operation: "Funny thing about baseball. Most executives of the game are more peeved at Curt Flood, for his stand against the reserve clause than they are at Denny McLain for his outside dealings that caused him to be suspended from the game until July. Poor Denny, as Commissioner Bowie Kuhn stated last week, is just an ignorant $200,000 (with outside interests) a year player who was used by unscrupulous outside parties. Flood, on the other hand, has been described as an ungrateful you know what, who is trying to destroy the very foundation of the game. Now how about that for making good old American common sense!"[46] (McLain was suspended for three months of the 1970 season. Flood was never suspended for suing baseball, and since he attempted a comeback in 1971, it can even be said that he was not quite black-listed from the game either) Several members of the black press praised Flood because he was fighting for a principle at great sacrifice. Bill Nunn Jr. wrote: "That is why I believe Flood should be commended for the battle he is waging. He isn't doing it for personal gain. He's fighting for something he believes in. Few men are willing to pick up the sword of battle under such circumstances."[47] Nunn added: "Even if you don't agree with Curt Flood in his fight against organized baseball concerning the reserve clause, his fortitude in fighting for what he believes to be right has to be admired. Flood thus joins a growing list of black athletes who have placed principle above personal gain. Jackie Robinson was one of the first when he quit organized baseball rather [than] join a new club after being traded by the Brooklyn Dodgers. Others who come to mind [are] Cassius (Muhammad Ali) Clay, Jim Brown, Arthur Ashe, and Bill Russell."[48] Civil rights leader and nonviolent draft resister Bayard Rustin also compared Flood to other noted black athletes who stood up to the system in his column that appeared in *The Philadelphia Tribune:* "[Flood's suit] is also an attempt to reform an institution in which black athletes have acquired prestige and wealth and have become a source of pride for other Negroes. As such, Flood stands in the tradition of such black athletes as Jackie Robinson and Muhammad Ali who, in addition to achieving great status within their professions, took courageous stands on issues of human rights."[49] Ric Roberts compared Flood to other black baseball players who rebelled in a somewhat different way, as a kind of Samson whose destruction of the temple becomes a form of self-destruction: "To all intents and purposes, Jackie Robinson's stardusted career lost its glitter, never to gleam again from that hour, between the 1954 and 1955 seasons when he put the finger on what he called the biased anti-Negro front office of the then reigning New York Yankees. From the moment Larry Doby dropped Yankee pitcher Al Ditmar, with a sizzling left hook in the summer of 1958, Larry's big league career was finished—forever. We mention Jackie and Larry, of course, because they led the black parade—from the top black administered baseball, into the majors. Baseball's punitive code struck both men down. Unless Flood is the seventh son of a seventh son, the obit index rests upon the ex-St. Louis Cardinals star."[50] Sports editor Jess Peters Jr., in his column, countered the argument that a man who makes $90,000 cannot be a slave: "The fact that major league baseball players are fairly well paid during their big league careers is really irrelevant; anyone who follows a normal path of logic can't ignore the fact that a man who makes $20,000 a year is entitled to no less Constitutional protection than a man who makes $5,000."[51] *Ebony* magazine praised Flood in a photo-editorial in which he was called, in connection to the slavery claim made against the reserve clause, the Abe Lincoln of baseball.[52] "It will be a bit of poetic justice," the editorial continued, "should it turn out that a black man finally brings freedom and democracy to baseball. After all, organized baseball kept black players out of the game for seventy-five years just because they were black."

What is clear is that the black press generally saw Flood in heroic terms, as a fighter for principle, as someone unafraid to challenge a white-dominated system, and as someone who was in the tradition of important, politically conscious black athletes. His argument about the reserve clause being a violation of the Thirteenth Amendment fell upon sympathetic ears, although it should not be assumed that all blacks, because of their common history of slavery and oppressive treatment at the hands of whites, would be supportive of Flood's involuntary servitude claim or would see it as sensible. I encountered more than a few black men at the time of Flood's case who thought he was a fool and should have played in Philadelphia. "Where else is he going to make that kind of money? There are few places where a black man can. Besides, you can't beat the white man at a game that he has rigged in his favor. He should go out there and play and let a white boy beat that reserve clause in court or let the union do it." More than a few blacks did not find paternalism nearly as abhorrent as Flood. I occasionally heard this opinion: "He should be grateful to the white man for being able to make that kind of money playing a game. There are no black people who can pay him that kind of money for doing anything, legal or illegal." But criticism of this sort was expressed by many blacks about Ali's decision not to join the army, yet Ali became the kind of political symbol for blacks during the 1960s and 1970s that Flood never did.

And Flood, over the years since the case was decided, has not become a politicized sports hero for new generations of blacks in the way Ali and Jackie Robinson have. (I recall few special tributes to Flood in black publications when he died in 1997 and few public expressions of sorrow by black public figures or leaders.) I think the reason for this is very much related to the nature of Flood's battle. He was fighting a particular legal advantage that baseball owners had that was not explicitly racial. In other words, what was done to Flood, in trading him to Philadelphia against his will, was not done to him because he was black, nor was it something that was only done to black players. And Flood did have the choice of continuing his career in Philadelphia for a higher salary than what he was being paid in St. Louis. Both Ali's and Robinson's struggles seemed more racial because their experiences seemed unique, something that could only happen to black men. Even Ali's legal battle against the draft seemed more dramatic, because for the black public there was more at stake. Ali was fighting his government, not a small cartel of businessmen in a tiny industry called baseball. If Flood failed, then he was, at worst, out of a job in major league baseball; if Ali failed, then he would be imprisoned, which seemed far worse and far more political to most blacks. In Robinson's case, his struggle to integrate baseball made him the emblem of his race. If Robinson failed, many blacks felt, then the whole race failed (although this was not, in point of fact, strictly true). Flood's case carried not any of this resonance; if Flood failed, then there was nothing much at stake for blacks at large. In this regard, despite the fact that Flood was generally more sympathetically received in the black community, he may have been more intensely admired and supported by those whites who truly found the entrenched power of baseball owners utterly detestable and who would be especially fond of a black rebel going against the system because of its richer symbolic potential. Flood would be more the darling of the white liberal Left than he would ever be of the black civil rights establishment or of black nationalist-minded thinkers.

One of Flood's most persistent critics was *St. Louis Post-Dispatch* sportswriter Bob Broeg, who wrote several columns about the Flood case. Broeg was never convinced by Flood's claim that the reserve clause reduced a player to involuntary servitude, which he thought went to the heart of the issue of Flood's entire case. The headlines for his columns tell the story: "$100,000 a Year—What a Way To Be Mistreated,"[53] "Does 'Principle' or 'Principal' Motivate Flood?"[54] and "Sports Get Jilted When Athletes Go A-courting."[55] Broeg's criticism of Flood's legal claims against the reserve clause includes the following: First, that a man who collects Flood's kind of salary cannot possibly be considered a peon or a slave in any rational sense of the term, and if he is being more than fairly compensated for his services, then how can he claim to be a slave? The basic issue of the unfairness of slavery, as nearly everyone understands it, is not being compensated for one's labor, to have someone unfairly take one's labor through coercion or force. None of that, in Broeg's mind, existed in the Flood case. Broeg said that he would have been more sympathetic to a challenge to the reserve clause if it had been made by a less affluent player.[56] Second, the Cardinals had rendered much aid to Flood "above and beyond the call of contractual obligations, with financial and personal problems of which he must still be aware, yet he does not choose to mention or acknowledge."[57] This, for Broeg, is tantamount to lack of loyalty to the organization on Flood's part. Moreover, if Broeg's contentions are true, then Flood misrepresented aspects of the nature of his relationship with the organization, so the fact that he was informed about the trade with an abrupt phone call did not characterize the true nature of the organization's support for him during the years he played for it. Broeg might even have gone farther with this line of reasoning and argued that Flood's initial reaction to the trade showed that he was disappointed that the organization showed so little gratitude for his services, the very thing he was accusing the organization of wanting from him in some manipulative way. Finally, Broeg argued that the reserve clause had changed over time, as had the status of the ballplayer: at the time of Flood's suit the players had a good pension plan, they had rules about how deeply their salaries could be cut, and they benefited from changes in roster construction, the draft, and interleague trading that made their life a great deal better than it had been.[58]

But in some respects it could be argued that Broeg's arguments are really nothing more than an elaborate rehearsal of the theme of ingratitude. The Cardinals had been good to Flood, so why should Flood wish to be free? What Broeg does not account for in his argument is the fact that the Cardinals traded Flood, and this is what Flood objects to, not how the Cardinals treated him up to the time of the trade. And if, indeed, the Cardinals did not want him, then why should Flood not be able to go where he wished instead of where the Cardinals wanted him to go? For the argument of paternalism, as it was conceived by the slave owners of the nineteenth century, the slave was taken care of; families, contrary to abolitionists such as Mrs. Stowe, were not broken up—the slave was indeed part of the larger, fictive plantation family, hence the degrading honorific titles "aunt" and "uncle." What Flood was arguing in his objection to the trade was that the Cardinals wanted all of the binding human obligations of paternalism when they wanted the player and all of the freedom of the commodities market when they did not. Flood's challenge, for Broeg, thwarted the logic of paternalism, but paternalism has only the logic of power for the paternalist and the logic of obedience for the recipient. That Broeg added the point about favors done for Flood above and beyond the terms of his contract only means that Broeg believed that paternalism not only has a logic but also a morality or an internal set of ethical demands upon the parties bound by it. But, in truth, no real morality can exist in paternalism, for the system only replicates and reflects how well those who control it mask their ability to do so with favors, concessions, and pet treatment of star players, how well they mask their power through, paradoxically, the whimsical exercise of it as an expression of benevolence or indulgence. The exceptionalist status granted baseball by its being allowed the reserve clause was part and parcel, reification, of the broader exceptionalist status that the sport enjoyed that gave it its mythical standing in American society. This was because the exceptionalism of baseball mirrored and interpreted the exceptionalism of America itself, in that it demanded gratitude from the players for being permitted to play the sport in much the same way the country had, at times, such as during the era of cold war liberalism; demanded gratitude and loyalty from its citizens for being able to live here, as in the American South, the exceptionalist region of our country; and demanded gratitude from blacks in their debilitating paternalism that insisted, with Orwellian logic, that slavery and degradation were freedom and uplift. In the velvet glove of the myth of baseball as the Great American pastime the game of heroes, the sport that symbolized our democratic impulses, was the iron fist of its absolutist corporate power, a power that the sport enjoyed far too long in the form of the unrestrained exercise of its reserve clause. It is much to the credit of labor organizing and our legal system that, after the failure of the Flood challenge, the situation in baseball significantly changed for the better for the players.

3

Donovan McNabb, Rush Limbaugh, and the Making of the Black Quarterback

THE CONTROVERSY involving conservative radio commentator Rush Limbaugh and former Philadelphia Eagles quarterback Donovan McNabb began on Sunday, September 28, 2003, at which time, and for several years following, McNabb was the face of the Eagles franchise. Limbaugh, who had been hired that season by ESPN to do commentary for their Sunday morning pre-game show, "Sunday NFL Countdown," said on the air, in response to the question of whether McNabb was regressing in the early days of 2003, that he thought McNabb was overrated, that is, was given more credit for his team's success than he deserved and was overesteemed beyond what his performance on the field merited. "Sorry to say this, I don't think [McNabb's] been that good from the get-go. I think what we've had here is a little social concern in the NFL. The media has [*sic*] been very desirous that a black quarterback do well, black coaches and black quarterbacks doing well. There is a little hope invested in McNabb, and he got a lot of credit for the performance of this team that he didn't deserve. The defense carried this team."[1] In the story of the black NFL quarterback, it is difficult to tell if Limbaugh's remark is the beginning of the end or merely the end of a very long beginning.

THE PASSER VERSUS THE POLEMICIST

It was the way Limbaugh framed his critique that caused the problem. Had Limbaugh said no more than he thought that McNabb was overrated and that the defense carried the Eagles, the remark would have passed not quite unnoticed, for such a remark is meant to provoke some response, but certainly as nothing especially interesting to the world outside of rabid football fans, as it is virtually a commonplace in sports reporting to judge, assess, and reassess the performance and rankings of professional athletes. And it is one sure way for a commentator or a writer to get noticed, if not precisely benefiting his or her subject, if he or she says that some star player is not as good as he or she is cracked up to be. We might try to speculate why it is an important ritual in discussing sports to deflate an athlete's reputation. Of course it happens everywhere in the world of art, even in the realm of scientists and intellectuals, so why not sports? Perhaps in sports it is a form of masculine contest. Perhaps it is simply a human need to expose something that we think is phony, the emperor-has-no-clothes syndrome. Perhaps it is envy; after all, the critic, who cannot perform at a level nor earn a salary even close to his or her subject (Limbaugh is an exception here, as he is a very wealthy man), can reduce the mighty athlete by a mere utterance. It is the nature of public performance to generate criticism, particularly in sports, the intricacies and technicalities of which seem self-evidently understandable to fans. And Rush Limbaugh was speaking for the fan and in the guise of a passionate follower, one of the fancy, as it might have been called back in the days of bare-knuckle prizefighting.

Limbaugh has always been sports crazy: he played football in high school, worked for the Kansas City Royals baseball team, and fell in love with the Pittsburgh Steelers when he lived in Pittsburgh during the team's glory years of the early 1970s. Besides, as Limbaugh's biographer points out, football was especially identified as the game of Republicans in the 1970s, the game of Richard Nixon and Gerald Ford, the game of metaphorical warfare. "The anti-war left despised the NFL, with its long bombs and ground attacks and martial values."[2] Anyone familiar with Limbaugh's radio program knows that he considers leftism not only an ideology but also an aesthetic, a taste culture, which he loves to satirize as pretentious. For Limbaugh liberalism is a form of snobbery and self-righteousness. So the fact that many leftists do not like football almost certainly would appeal to him as a conservative who loves football.

The world of sports reporting and sports evaluation for the general public relies greatly on grandiose statements of praise or harsh counterstatements of criticism that border, sometimes, on invective or insensitivity. In this back-and-forth swing of ultra-language to invest a seemingly meaningless activity with urgency, relevance, and even mythology, there is nothing unusual about a player being seen as both great and mediocre simultaneously. The sheer tension of this ambivalence about some players is part of what gives sports their energy and power, their attraction, for fans. This tension is also what makes the opinions of sports commentators, who represent both the nosiness of the person with the inside dope and the crafted taste of the aficionado, relevant. The power of sports is about the passion of the mind that can be evoked to make a contrived contest mean something or to be worthy of someone's attention. The power of sports is precisely located in its ability to make the public care about the outcome, which means that the public is emotionally invested, if only momentarily, in the people who create that outcome. The sports commentator serves as a facilitator to that end: to help make the public care, to make success and failure, sometimes ambiguous in sports, something of the nature of a myth or an epic and also something of a moral issue. High-performance athletes are not like other people: Did the winner *deserve* to win? If a performer fails, has he or she not squandered his or her talents, and so, in a fundamental way, does not deserve to have them or is not worthy of the magnitude of his or her gifts? Or if the talent has been exaggerated, has he or she not, in some way, committed fraud on the public, played a con game?

But Limbaugh did not simply say that McNabb was overrated. He said that McNabb was overrated because white liberal sportswriters and broadcasters very much wanted him to succeed in a position that, historically, blacks rarely played in the NFL. This caused such a firestorm of outrage in certain quarters that within forty-eight hours Limbaugh was forced to resign from ESPN. Limbaugh was accused of being racist, and it would not be the last time he would be so accused, nor the last time he would be publicly embarrassed by having to give up his aspiration to become associated with professional football. (I discuss the latter incident, which occurred in 2009, later in this chapter.) He insisted that his remarks carried "no racist intent whatsoever." He went on to say, on his radio show, that the overwhelming reaction to his remarks was proof that he had said something that must have had some truth, something that had hit some social and political nerve.

In reporting on the first game McNabb played after Limbaugh's comments, on Sunday, October 5, in Philadelphia against the Washington Redskins, the next day the *New York Times* headlined the article "McNabb Issues His Reply," and writer Thomas George wrote that the Eagles' victory gave "a definitive answer to the question of whether their quarterback, Donovan McNabb, was overrated."[3] The writer then went on to say that McNabb's response was "157 passing yards, 18 more rushing and his first touchdown pass of the season." It was curious that these statistics were seen as "a definitive answer" to Limbaugh's claim that McNabb was over-rated when they were, in fact, not especially impressive. McNabb completed half of his passes and threw two interceptions; so-so completion rates and interceptions bedeviled him for the first several Eagles games of 2003. Neither of these facts was mentioned in the article, an odd omission, as one of McNabb's interceptions set up one of Washington's touchdowns. Also, McNabb was not responsible for all of the Eagles' scores, as one of their touchdowns was scored by their defense. One hundred fifty-seven yards is not a noteworthy total for a quarterback when an outstanding day is typically throwing 250 yards or more. Eighteen yards rushing is negligible: an in-the-pocket quarterback may manage that much. McNabb, known at least until this point in his career as a scrambling or running quarterback, actually did not run very much in 2003 and certainly had had better days than that. (McNabb ran 355 yards in 2003 averaging 5 yards per carry in sixteen games; in 2002 he ran 460 yards and averaged 7.3 yards per carry in ten games in an injury-shortened season. He was injured in game eleven but returned to his position as quarterback during the Eagles' play-off run. His running, though, has decreased as the years have passed, probably due to a combination of age and the cumulative effect of injuries. In the early years of his career, McNabb played in games where he was virtually his team's leading rusher. In this sense, he was reminiscent of the Eagles first star black quarterback, Randall Cunningham, whom I shall discuss momentarily.) Finally, the Eagles barely won this game against the Redskins; the final score was 27 to 25. The article contained several quotations about how McNabb dealt with Limbaugh's comments, including one from McNabb himself, almost as though Limbaugh's comments were an injury he had to overcome in order to play. One might argue that McNabb, after all, has had to deal with greater adversity, for instance, when he played a game in 2002 with a broken ankle, a career-threatening bit of derring-do, or when he had to withstand the crush of media attention during the Eagles play-off runs in 2000, 2001, and 2002, a severe distraction. One might expect a professional athlete, as indeed he is a public figure, to take criticism, whatever its merit or source, more or less as a matter of course. Moreover, no good athlete, and McNabb is certainly a gifted athlete, is supposed to let what is said about him, or even what may be happening in his personal life, affect his performance on the field. High-performance athletes like McNabb are, indeed, so insulated from the world and the normal responsibilities of adulthood that they often suffer from a debilitating form of immaturity that makes it easy for people to take advantage of them.[4] They are taught to be concerned only with their performance, which in the pressurized world in which they live becomes their only reality. It would, in fact, be a sign that McNabb lacked "mental toughness" had Limbaugh's remarks, or the storm that these remarks created, affected his performance.

But the October 6 *New York Times* article assumed that the Limbaugh criticism was of a special and, apparently, a different order than the sort that McNabb had any right to expect. Perhaps the writer of the piece found it especially unnerving that Limbaugh criticized McNabb by mentioning race, but McNabb could not have gone as far as he has in his profession, playing the particular position he has played, without having to deal with race as an issue. Blacks as quarterbacks, particularly in the NFL, have been so fraught with political and cultural implications of such wide significance that director Oliver

Stone made a movie about the drama, *Any Given Sunday* (1999), featuring a scrambling black quarterback, an aging white quarterback, and a white coach.[5] This was, for Stone, the love triangle of American sports. On one level, at least from the perspective of blacks, the drama of the black quarterback concerns the black male's ability to lead (which dates back to the politics surrounding the making of black officers in the American military); on another level it concerns an African American taking a job away from a white, taking a job that had been defined as a white job, and from the perspective of some whites, that smacks of affirmative action, the redistribution of goods at the expense of the dominant group, a contentious public policy that has been in place for the last thirty years. Two questions arise from this view of the issue: Can a black successfully play the position *in the way that the position needs to be played?* And, should he?

Limbaugh could have used this *New York Times* article to demonstrate the thing he asserted. McNabb could reasonably be seen in this piece to have gotten special consideration on the part of the writer, as he was rather excessively praised for not having had a particularly impressive game, and it seemed as though his race had something to do with it. Why should

McNabb get a form of special pleading or cheer-leading by a *Times* sports reporter because both the writer and McNabb felt McNabb suffered some racial insult, as though that makes life tougher for him than for anybody else in his line of work? The assumption is, of course, that having to endure racial insults, real or perceived, does make life tougher for minorities, as the historically persecuted are referred to in the United States, and so they must be protected from it. This once led writer Stanley Crouch to muse out loud to me about how black people managed to survive as a people before white liberal opinion thought them too sensitive or vulnerable to endure or ignore seemingly racist remarks. In other words, there might be something a bit condescending in the effort of the *Times* writer to help McNabb weather the storm of snide or casual racial remarks.

In the same October 6 edition of the *New York Times*, TV sports columnist Richard Sandomir wrote a piece about ESPN's response to Limbaugh's remarks. Several accounts noted that when Limbaugh made his remarks on the air the other commentators did not take him to task for what he said about the media's overrating McNabb because McNabb was black. Chris Berman, the host of the show, originally said that he did not believe that Limbaugh's tone or intent was malicious. "As cut and dried as it seems in print, I didn't think so when it went by my ears. I probably should have looked to soften it. We're sorry we upset a guy who got off to a rough start," Berman said.[6] In Sandomir's article, Berman, on the apology edition of "Sunday NFL Countdown," is quoted as saying, "I'm angry because it hurt African Americans. I'm angry for the hurt it's caused all people. I've never looked at Donovan McNabb as a black quarterback. Ever. I missed it. I shouldn't have missed it. I've been kicking myself all week. In truth, we all missed it."[7] The two black commentators on the show—Tom Jackson and Michael Irvin—both former NFL players, were mentioned in news pieces about the incident for not responding to Limbaugh. As Sandomir wrote, "Tom Jackson, who is the program's senior analyst, and who is black, took the brunt [of the] criticism for not rebutting Limbaugh." Jackson is quoted as saying, "It was not our decision to have Rush Limbaugh on this show." He continued: "Rush Limbaugh is known for the divisive nature of his rhetoric. . . . A player in this league who has a young son called me this week, and his son now wants to know if it's all right for blacks to play quarterback.

Rush Limbaugh's comment could not have been more hurtful." He said Limbaugh "broke the trust" he had promised to honor when he was hired when he injected social commentary into the program. "He was brought in to talk football."[8] Sandomir then goes on to say that the show's executives needed to apologize as well: "Where was George Bodenheimer, the president of ESPN, or Mark Shapiro, the executive vice president, who has led the company's headlong leap into entertainment? Undoubtedly, Limbaugh's hiring was done for entertainment's sake, to get more writers to take notice of the program outside of the sports realm. It is reasonable to assume that ESPN believed people would tune in to find out what wacky thing Limbaugh would say next."[9]

At that time this all seemed rather strange for Sandomir to write. I was under the impression that professional football was, in fact, entertainment, so how could ESPN have taken a "headlong leap into entertainment"? To be sure, sports are distinct from other forms of entertainment, depending on the drama of producing an unpredictable, unscripted outcome, and athletes represent a different sort of symbolic figure than other pop culture figures. Nonetheless, I thought ESPN was nothing but entertainment, selling sports as a diversion. And it seemed curious to me to hire someone like Rush Limbaugh, a noted conservative polemicist and political observer, to add "entertainment" to an entertainment show. Of course, one could argue that all radio talk shows—from Drs. Joy Browne and Laura Schlesinger to Rush Limbaugh and Tavis Smiley— are forms of entertainment, and that would not be untrue, but they are also something else. Limbaugh's show was the highest rated talk show in the country, with an audience nearly three times larger than his closest competitor. ESPN probably hoped that some of those people would tune in not to hear "what wacky thing Limbaugh would say next" but, rather, to hear what insight he would bring to the show, as most of Limbaugh's audience was apt to share his opinions and respect his judgment. Clearly Limbaugh's legions of liberal detractors were hoping, even expecting, that he would say something stupid, but the millions who love him do not consider him stupid. And both liberals and conservatives realize that while Limbaugh is a satirist, he is neither a clown nor a comedian in any conventional sense. Part of what ESPN wanted from Limbaugh was something more than mere football analysis— indeed, they might have reasonably expected some social commentary about the significance of it all from a man who makes a living from social and political commentary. As Allen Barra wrote for *Slate*: "If they didn't hire Rush Limbaugh to say things like this, what did they hire him for? To talk about the prevent defense?"[10] There were already people on the show who were more than qualified to talk about the prevent defense, running stunts, the limitations of Cover 2, the likelihood of a quarterback on a third and long setting up a screen play to counteract a blitz, and the effectiveness of play-action passes when one's ground game is nonexistent. Part of the fun for football fans would have been hearing Limbaugh discuss this sort of thing, but part of the attraction also was to hear *what else* he was going to say beyond the Xs and Os. It might be said that on a show of experts (and sports programs pride themselves on their display of expertise), Limbaugh was the expert controversialist.

Indeed, hiring Limbaugh was ESPN's attempt to suggest that football had some wider meaning beyond the obsession of the passionate fan. Whatever promise Limbaugh may have made about not making social commentary, his presence itself signified social commentary of some sort or another. The man's claim to fame in our society is his political opinions, not his expertise to analyze football, for which he may or may not possess competence. There is no question that Limbaugh possesses passion—he is America's most famous, most forthright, and most combative conservative. What Sandomir was trying to suggest in his article was that Limbaugh was both significant (he is famous, after all, for his opinions) and insignificant (his politics are really "entertainment," and he is apt to say "wacky" things; of course, the question is, wacky to whom?) in the same instance. But his politics are not just entertainment, for if they were, then people, including three Democratic presidential candidates of the day—Howard Dean, Wesley Clark, and Al Sharpton—would not have reacted so fiercely to what he said about McNabb to score points with their constituencies. To be sure Limbaugh almost certainly did not mean the remark to be mere entertainment, and the remark may have struck the public and the pundits in many ways, but "wacky" was not one of them.

It also seemed odd that the two black commentators on the show were identified in several news articles as deserving special censure because they did not challenge Limbaugh when he spoke, did not, to use the parlance of the street, come to the aid of a

stricken brother, if McNabb can be so characterized. But let us remember exactly what Limbaugh
said: he said that it was the media, that is, the white
liberal media, that overrated McNabb because they
wanted to see a black quarterback succeed. In other
words, Limbaugh was accusing the white media of
liberal racism. It seems that anyone could have responded to that, indeed, that whites might be more
moved to respond, as it was directed at the fact that
they control the images of athletes and how people
think about them. Chris Berman, the show's host,
was in a much better position to respond than anyone else, but when he first heard the remark he did
not notice anything wrong with it. White ex-football
players were on the show as well. In the matter of a
black quarterback being overrated, why couldn't
Steve Young, an ex-quarterback, who was also, like
McNabb, a scrambler, and who certainly ought to
have known how quarterbacks are seen by the press,
have responded? Why was it just the moral burden of
the black commentators to respond to Limbaugh?

Of course many white sportswriters did take the
bait and respond, such as *St. Louis Post-Dispatch*
sports editor Bernie Miklasz, on October 2, 2003,
who agreed with Limbaugh that McNabb was overrated but that race had nothing to do with it. Mik-

lasz argued that McNabb was overrated because the Eagles had made him the second pick in the first round of the 1999 draft. "With that entry comes intense hype, great expectations, high standards, and to fulfill the hopes cast for him, McNabb would have to play brilliantly and take his team to the Super Bowl, and maybe even win the Super Bowl." Miklasz continued: "If you're the second pick in the draft, and heralded as a franchise savior, you'd better deliver sensational results, and that's true of any quarterback, black or white. McNabb is not more or less overrated than Cleveland's Tim Couch, or San Diego's Drew Brees—two acclaimed white quarterback draftees who haven't made a major impact on their teams."[11]

Miklasz could have said that in 1999 McNabb was one of five quarterbacks drafted in the first round, an unusually high number. So he was not unique in regard to expectations. He was drafted behind Tim Couch but ahead of Daunte Culpepper of Minnesota and Akili Smith of Cincinnati, both black. On the other hand, McNabb's career quarterback rating in 2003 was 77, which was somewhat better than Couch's 75.1 but less than Culpepper's 86.3. McNabb might have been overrated for a quarterback with that rating. One could make a case that because McNabb was a black quarterback who was a number two pick, the highest pick for a black quarterback between 1998 and 2003, with the exception of Virginia Tech quarterback Michael Vick as the number one pick in 2001, at least some sportswriters might have wanted to see him succeed because of the combination of his skin color and his being such a high pick. So on the whole Miklasz's argument about McNabb's draft position, and the high expectations it elicited, did not preclude, by any means, that race played a role in the making of McNabb's professional reputation. But did the white press want him to succeed more than, say, the late Steve McNair, a black quarterback who was drafted by Tennessee in 1995 as the third pick of the draft and who had a career rating in 2003 of 83.3, better than McNabb's? Had the press pushed McNair as well? McNair's career bears a number of similarities to McNabb's: coming to a team that had had a superior black quarterback before (Warren Moon), playing for many years with one team and a head coach who was hired when McNair was drafted, a running quarterback (in 1997, he rushed for over 600 yards) who stopped doing so as he aged, leading his team to several play-off berths and one Super Bowl, and playing in several Pro Bowls. Had

Limbaugh said that McNair was overrated because he was black, would the reaction have been the same?

When new head coach Andy Reid drafted McNabb in 1999, many in Philadelphia were vehement in expressing their disappointment. Those present at the draft booed the choice. The football fans in Philadelphia wanted the Eagles to draft Ricky Williams, a black running back from the University of Texas, so the disappointment does not seem racial unless one were to assume that had the Eagles taken Couch the fans would have been happier because they thought him more appropriate as a franchise quarterback. And Williams was, after all, playing a traditional and an overwhelmingly "black" position in football. As their careers panned out, Philadelphia fans would have been far unhappier with Couch, who was essentially a bust as a NFL quarterback. (Akili Smith was also a bust, unable to master the Cincinnati Bengals' playbook.) The Philly fans would have been even unhappier with Williams, who has had his problems, including inconsistent play, several drug suspensions, and no leadership skills. The fans in Philly had had two starting black quarterbacks in the 1990s, Randall Cunningham and Rodney Peete, neither of whom took the team to the Super Bowl or seemed capable of winning big play-off games. By the time of the McNabb draft, had at least some of the fans become a bit suspicious of black quarterbacks?

THE COMING OF RANDALL CUNNINGHAM

I was saved in 1987 and, believe it or not, it happened at Spanish Trails, a golf course in Las Vegas—which ironically is nicknamed "Sin City." I was with Tommy Cameron, a friend from my college days, and after we were finished playing 18 holes and were walking toward the car, Tommy asked, "Have you been saved?"

I said I didn't know. "What does being saved mean?" Tommy explained and asked if I wanted to be saved and I asked how long would it take.

—Randall Cunningham[12]

Cunningham, who was drafted in the second round by the Eagles out of the University of Nevada–Las Vegas in 1985, was a popular player during his glory years in a script that seemed similar to Stone's *Any Given Sunday*. Cunningham—who could run, throw, and punt—arrived as a backup to aging white quarterback Ron Jaworski, who had, five years earlier, taken the Eagles to Super Bowl XV, a loss to the Oakland Raiders of 27 to 10, which would be the team's only Super Bowl appearance until McNabb led them to Super Bowl XXXIX in 2005. Cunningham was an unorthodox, scrambling quarterback, Jaworski a traditional in-the-pocket passer. Coach Marion Campbell, the Swamp Fox, drafted Cunningham, which was a bit of a surprise, as Cunningham was so unconventional and considered quite risky, but Eagles offensive Ted Marchibroda liked the fact that the young quarterback was so different, thinking perhaps that he could be a unique weapon as a quarterback; indeed, within a few years (September 11, 1989), Cunningham was featured on the cover of *Sports Illustrated* as "The Ultimate Weapon" and "The Quarterback of the '90s." At first matters were difficult, as old quarterback mentor Sid Gilman could do nothing with Cunningham, not even get him to look at game film (shades of Willie Beamen, the black quarterback of Stone's *Any Given Sunday!*),[13] but Gilman left when Campbell was fired.

Then, in 1986, Chicago Bears defensive coordinator Buddy Ryan became the Eagles new head coach. He began using Cunningham in third-down-and-long situations, taking advantage of the young quarterback's remarkable scrambling abilities.

When Jaworski was injured, Cunningham became the starter, a job he was to keep until he became a backup to Rodney Peete in 1995. Cunningham enjoyed playing under Ryan, who ran a fairly undisciplined team. The Eagles' defense developed a "gangsta" reputation with a "body bag" mentality and piled up penalties. When the intimidation worked, led by Seth Joyner, Andre Waters, Reggie White, and Clyde Simmons, the Eagles had a fearsomely effective defense. When it did not work, the defense was just vicious, uncontrolled, and burned on big plays. Cunningham was expected to "come up with four or five big plays a game—either throwing or running the football."[14] As Ryan said about Cunningham, "I don't want to make him a stereotype quarterback, he's too good a football player."[15] Yet in many ways Cunningham became the stereotypic *black* quarterback, scrambling, making up plays on the fly, ignoring open receivers because he consistently failed to check off his receivers, and doing everything that was the antithesis of an in-the-pocket, white quarterback. For three years in a row, Cunningham led his team in rushing. He rushed for over 900 yards in 1990 alone. He was a Pro-Bowl player in three of his first five years in the NFL, so as a *black* quarterback, he was a resounding success on many levels. Cunningham called plays devised by the offensive coordinator (Ted Plumb) and the quarterback coach (Doug Scovill, to whom Cunningham was very close personally) but was given a great deal of latitude in how much he could run or improvise plays. "They gave me my freedom," Cunningham wrote, "and that's when I played my best."[16] In effect Ryan let Cunningham do whatever he wanted. And Cunningham reveled in being the *black*, scrambling quarterback: he called his company Scrambler Inc., his autobiography was called *I'm Still Scrambling*, and when he returned in 1992 from a blown-out knee, he wore a cap that read "I'm Back Scrambling." Tension first developed in 1990, when the Eagles hired Rich Kotite as the new offensive coordinator. Kotite wanted Cunningham to stop running and throw the ball more. He expected a completion rate of 70 percent, extraordinarily high. Before Kotite's arrival Cunningham never had a 60 percent completion rate, a benchmark for a superior quarterback. But in 1992, under Kotite, Cunningham achieved this 60 percent rate for a full season. However, Cunningham never really got along well with Kotite, who eventually became the Eagles' head coach, replacing Ryan in 1991. Another form of tension was that

Cunningham was far and away the most disliked player on the team; partly fueled by envy, partly by the inconsistency of his play, and partly by his unwillingness to learn his position thoroughly and professionally, as well as his incredible self-centeredness, his obsession with his own stats, and his complete unwillingness to socialize with his teammates, Cunningham existed in a bubble of his own making. Even the black players on the team disliked him, calling him "Ran-doll."[17] In 1995, Cunningham's last year in Philadelphia, he played under an African American head coach, as the Eagles hired Ray Rhodes, defensive coordinator of the 1994 Super Bowl champions, the San Francisco 49ers. Rhodes benched Cunningham, whose abilities had been hampered due to injuries, in favor of Rodney Peete, a black quarterback who was more conventional than Cunningham and who had largely been a backup throughout his career. The Eagles made the play-offs that year but were bounced in the second round. After 1995 Peete would return to the role of backup with the Eagles behind white quarterbacks Ty Detmer, Bobby Hoying, and Koy Detmer. Rhodes, having lost both the team's confidence and his own, was fired after the 1998 game when the Eagles went 3 and 13. How much the

Eagles' past history with black quarterbacks, or a black head coach, for that matter, affected how the fans initially reacted to McNabb is impossible to say. Was drafting McNabb, like hiring Rhodes, some form of affirmative action, some way for football to legitimate itself in twenty-first century America? Cunningham certainly broke new ground with local white fans with his success, but the team's failure to win a championship or even get very far in the play-offs may have also convinced many fans that a scrambling, "jitterbugging" black quarterback may not be the best option for a successful offense. From his initial reception, did McNabb himself maintain nagging doubts about the Philly fans' willingness to accept him as a top-flight quarterback? McNabb, in 2006, enduring a miserable season and guiding the Eagles to a losing record, was injured in the Eagles' eleventh game. Backup Jeff Garcia took the helm, miraculously leading the team to five straight wins, a division title, and the play-offs. Naturally Garcia became very popular with the fans, especially after the Eagles won in the first play-off round. McNabb's family thought that if the Eagles won the Super Bowl, even reached it, without McNabb that McNabb might be traded, and that he would surely be crucified in the press and during the sports call-in shows. Why keep McNabb if a backup could do as well, if not better? Now no one who knew anything about football thought that Garcia had anything even close to McNabb's skills and abilities, and it would have bordered on the irrational if the Eagles had traded McNabb had they reached the Super Bowl that year and replaced him with Garcia. The fact that McNabb's family thought that this might happen shows how unsure they were of McNabb's position in Philadelphia, despite his considerable success and, more generally, how blacks frequently think of their exceptional precariousness when they are leaders.[18]

So perhaps some sportswriters might have been especially supportive of McNabb because of the negative way he was originally received by the Philadelphia sporting public, or because of some complex misunderstanding or misappreciation that these sportswriters may have felt the fan base may have had with previous black quarterbacks. In fact what would be the matrices by which we may learn how and why a black quarterback is either overrated or unduly deprecated? One way would be by reading dozens of sports articles in local papers about McNabb, articles that covered a period of years, and carefully comparing them to articles about comparable quarterbacks in the local papers of other cities during the same period while also comparing national and local press coverage of Cunningham and Peete with their peers. Then one would have to listen to hours of tapes from sports radio shows to record and measure the nature of the commentary about various players, black and white, and figure out a way to compare what was said that was negative and what was said that was positive and to identify in some demographically useful way who said what. It is unlikely that Limbaugh ever did anything like this, to base his idea of being overrated on something empirical. But then again neither did Bernie Miklasz or any other sportswriter who wrote about a particular athlete being overrated, therefore, it is impossible to know exactly what "overrated" means. What fine line is crossed where an athlete ceases to be evaluated accurately and becomes overrated? By whom is someone overrated, and are some opinions more important than others, and by what measure and compared to what or whom? Are there degrees of overrating? Are some athletes more overrated than others? Are there built-in mechanisms that exist in sports evaluation to correct for overrating? How much does an athlete's individuality affect his being overrated? Does it matter whether an athlete is indeed overrated, since it is the job of the sporting press to make these performers larger than life, mythical in some way? The overrated athlete simply becomes another useful way to talk about failure and disappointment, both obsessions with most sports fan and the sporting press. Since a sportswriter's job is to make the meaningless matter, can it be said that high-performance sports themselves are overrated as cultural activities, as at least half of the American public has no interest in sports at all, and sports as an economic activity constitutes such a tiny portion of the American GDP that they could disappear without creating even a momentary bump of disruption? Athletes induce greater or lesser hopes or expectations, greater or lesser anticipation or confidence, all based on their past performances. In athletics, everyone is always assuming that the past is prologue. Sports fans thrive on and live for the mad, endless speculations about the future, fixated on prophecy, on who will win or lose; but everyone is also buried in the empirical tomb of past performance, the quantitative graveyard of the Ghosts of Athletic Greatness Gone By.

How to Be a Black Quarterback

Bryan Burwell, a black sportswriter for the *St. Louis Post-Dispatch*, wrote a far angrier column about the Limbaugh–McNabb affair. He called Limbaugh "a mean-spirited, liberal-bashing, feminist-bashing, gay-bashing, minority-bashing, blowhard, who spent a great deal of energy ripping everyone who doesn't look or think like him."[19] He goes on to quote from a list of racist statements that Limbaugh allegedly made that was compiled by Fairness & Accuracy in Reporting, ending by saying, in effect, that ESPN got what it deserved in hiring Limbaugh in the first place. (These quotations—Limbaugh said he never made most of them and defied anyone to produce a tape showing that he had—hurt him greatly in 2009.) McNabb's popularity and success are, according to Burwell, "filled with Pro Bowls, two trips to the NFC championship game and stats that say at times he was responsible for 70 percent of the team's offense." But those achievements would not mean that McNabb was not overrated. After all, as of 2003, he had never taken his team to the Super Bowl or won it, although many thought that the Eagles of 2002, particularly, were Super Bowl material. Also, McNabb missed nearly half of his team's games the previous year due to his broken ankle, and the team performed just as well without him, even when a third-string quarterback was substituted for him. This might have indicated that the Eagles' great strength was their defense, as Limbaugh said. Moreover, the fact that McNabb at times was 70 percent of his team's offense was not so much a sign of his greatness, it could be argued, but of the inadequacy and thinness of the Eagles' offensive squad.

Allen Barra, writing for *Slate*, on Thursday, October 2, 2003, was one of the few white sportswriters to agree with Limbaugh on both points about McNabb being overesteemed because the white sportswriting establishment wanted to see black quarterbacks succeed. "Limbaugh lost his job," Barra wrote, "for saying in public what many football fans and analysts have been saying privately for the past couple of seasons."[20] Barra points out that McNabb's offense never ranked higher than tenth in his three seasons before 2003, and that in two of those seasons it ranked seventeenth in a league of thirty-two teams. Through 2002 their defense, on the other hand, ranked in the top ten. (The Eagles ranked seventeenth in offense—yardage—in 2000 and 2001. In

2003, through September, they ranked thirty-first in offense—yardage. And by the end of 2003, they ranked eighteenth in offense in yards gained but twentieth in defense in yards yielded. They still won twelve of their sixteen regular-season games, but their defense was not necessarily the strongest aspect of their game.)

Barra then compared McNabb to Tampa Bay quarterback Brad Johnson, a veteran of ten years, and not highly regarded by analysts. Johnson's rating as a passer was higher than McNabb's, his statistics, all around, were better, and he had won a Super Bowl. "In terms of performance, many NFL quarterbacks should be ranked ahead of McNabb. But McNabb has represented something special to all of us since he started his first game in the NFL, and we all know what that is." Barra continued:

> Limbaugh is being excoriated for making race an issue in the NFL. This is hypocrisy. I don't know of a football writer who didn't regard the dearth of a black NFL quarterback as one of the most important issues of the late '80s and early '90s. (The topic really caught fire after 1988, when Doug Williams of the Washington Redskins became the first black quarterback to win a Super Bowl.)

So far, no black quarterback has been able to dominate a league in which the majority of the players are black. To pretend that many of us didn't want McNabb to be the best quarterback in the NFL because he's black is absurd. To say that we shouldn't root for a quarterback to win because he's black is every bit as nonsensical as to say that we shouldn't have rooted for Jackie Robinson to succeed because he was black.[21]

This sounds much like the reasoning that many whites use in explaining why they feel President Barack Obama must succeed for more than mere ideological reasons, because as a black in such a leadership position, it would be beneficial, socially and culturally, for the country as a whole, just as they believe that his failure would be disastrous for race relations and for the cause of multicultural-ism. Black leadership success is a social good, indeed, a social necessity. Interestingly, Rush Lim-baugh has stated emphatically, since Obama's election, that he wants the president to fail. Lim-baugh does not attach any social or cultural signifi-cance to the success of blacks in the United States other than confirming the fact that American de-mocracy is color blind—anyone who works hard enough can achieve what he or she wants if he or she has values and habits that tend toward success. Limbaugh would argue that to have special hope for black success is liberal racism or a form of paternalism. Liberals have correctly pointed out that conservatives have often argued that black individual failure is a reflection of the dysfunctional character of the group.

But despite this cheerleading from most white sportswriters (it would be reasonable to think that some would not want black quarterbacks to succeed for fear that they would completely remove any white presence from the field), it can be assumed that coaches and team owners did not start using black quarterbacks (slightly less than one-third of NFL teams had black starting quarterbacks in 2003) as some sort of social experiment but, presumably, because they felt they could win games with them. It is difficult to say whether Eagles coach Andy Reid would have drafted Tim Couch instead of McNabb if he had had the number one pick, but he probably could have traded up for the number one pick if he wanted to ensure that he got Couch. It would be safe to say that Reid thought he could win more games with McNabb. And he turned out to be right. But perhaps Reid thought he could win more games because of McNabb being black, because he possessed more, as it is said, "pure athleticism" than a white quarterback. After all, this is why no one finds any whites who play cornerback in the NFL, nor will there be any movement to bring them back in that position. Perhaps there is interest in black quarterbacks because, since so many of the players on the average football team are black, over 70 percent, it might make sense to have a black quarterback as well, as he might be better able to relate to the other players. (Randall Cunningham, of course, proved that this was not necessarily true.) But even that reason would still be largely driven by the desire to win and by the need for a certain type of efficiency.

Offensive schemes today may be able to take greater advantage of a quarterback who can run, but if quarterbacks on the whole are mostly required to throw the ball and read defenses, then isn't a team wasting a black player who can run by making him a quarterback? It is rather like the reluctance in baseball to make a black a pitcher if his speed can be used in the outfield. Some may recognize this as the rationale behind "stacking" certain team positions with blacks, for not making blacks quarterbacks in the past, and, indeed, for putting a black in any "speed and quickness" position that did not require much thinking. And there is the rub, as the quarterback is a thinking position, and many believed blacks were not intelligent enough to play the position well. Scrambling, and most black quarterbacks have been characterized as such, was, for many, proof that blacks could not play the position well, that they had "happy feet" and could not think "strategically" (this was the problem with Cunningham in Philadelphia) but only react "instinctively." In the age of diversity and affirmative action, a black would not accept being stigmatized as being unable to function as a leader who could think. The white liberal Left that, paradoxically, abhorred racial difference but also celebrated it would not accept a black being so stigmatized either, and many such people are in the writing and media trade, what one might call the "words and their meaning" industry.

Thus we have a perfect conflation of practicality meeting politics; football changed in a way that made the black quarterback—as a stylistic innovation— more useful in winning games at the same time that blacks themselves would no longer tolerate being shunted from the position and white liberals thought it a social imperative that a cultural category called "the black quarterback" should exist for political reasons rather akin to the objectives of affirmative action, as a way to delegitimate white supremacy, to delegitimate institutional racism. But for a sports scholar like John Hoberman, arguing over how many black quarterbacks should exist, and whether our sporting press is actively promoting them, is missing the point. From his perspective blacks are not stigmatized because they are not quarterbacks, they are stigmatized because they are largely known in the United States through their achievement in athletics, in popular culture, and are not taken seriously as people who think seriously and deeply.[22] And the public generally does not perceive the performance of sports as any sort of profound exercise or demonstration of analytical or critical thinking, even in football, a highly strategized sport (thus the appellation "dumb jock"). Arguing whether African Americans should be this or that type of sports performer is merely splitting hairs. They remain entertainers in the end, a fact about which they themselves feel strongly ambivalent. And what *Any Given Sunday* showed was that blacks are now becoming quarterbacks because they are better entertainers at this position than white men. Is the real issue here whether football is more entertaining if black men are quarterbacks, or whether blacks remain stigmatized, seen as inferior, because of their success in sports, an exciting, highly elitist, but trivial aspect of American culture? What would blacks be if amateur and professional sports in America disappeared tomorrow, an ever-more troublesome race of the maladjusted, out of synch and unnecessary in a postindustrial society?

MORE BLACK RESPONSES TO LIMBAUGH

Like Bryan Burwell's column, black responses to Limbaugh are about what one would expect. J. C. Watts, quarterback at the University of Oklahoma and the Canadian Football League and Republican congressman from Oklahoma from 1995 to 2003, found Limbaugh's remarks "baffling." The criticism struck him as undeserved: "Why Donovan? I mean, his statistics, his performance, his leadership just did not merit those comments."[23] But conservatives commonly cast aspersions on the motives of the Left—which Limbaugh was doing in castigating the white press—by calling into question its judgments about blacks, by implying that mediocrity was being palmed off on the public as excellence. This may not have been Limbaugh's intention—he conceded that he thought McNabb was a good player—but it was often his effect, an effect that African Americans greatly resented and feared. Watts is right; most white quarterbacks in the NFL would be proud to have McNabb's statistics.

The two most striking black responses to the McNabb–Limbaugh affair were op-ed pieces written by John McWhorter and Jesse Jackson. Jackson, writing in the *Chicago Sun-Times* on October 7, 2003, said that Limbaugh's "poisonous words reveal much about the race-baiting politics so prevalent on the right." He went on to describe McNabb as "one of the modern mobile quarterbacks who [has] revolutionized the position." Jackson added that "Rush didn't see McNabb as an Eagle or as a quarterback. He saw him, first and foremost, as a black man." Jackson felt Limbaugh's comments were racist and incorrect for three reasons. First, he argued that blacks have never been pampered as quarterbacks but have had to overcome "entrenched prejudice to play [the position] at the professional level." Jackson was correct in saying that blacks who had been quarterbacks in college or high school had routinely been made into defensive backs or wide receivers. Second, he argued that Limbaugh was slurring black ability by implying that affirmative action was the reason McNabb was a quarterback, which is also tantamount to smearing affirmative action itself. Third, he argued that Limbaugh was after his favorite conservative bugaboo, "the liberal media." But Jackson also argued that "sports columnists tend to be bottom-line oriented. Win and you are the toast of the town. Lose and you're trash."

McWhorter, author of *Losing the Race: Self-Sabotage in Black America* (2000), wrote in the *New York Times* on October 4, 2003, that Limbaugh "has injected a bit of honesty into our public discourse about race . . . he raises a valid point: America wants to see black people succeed, whether they need help or not, and that yearning—with all its ambiguous and even adverse effects—has become part of the warp and woof of our national consciousness." McWhorter went on to say that if Limbaugh had made the remarks on his radio show and not on "Sunday NFL Countdown," then they would have gone unnoticed. He continued: "Limbaugh's mention of the possibility that McNabb is overrated because of his skin color is not racist in the least. Limbaugh certainly didn't claim that black people are not good at sports (that'd be a tough one to defend). Nor did he link his unenthusiastic view of McNabb's talents to his being black. He simply stated his view that the broader evaluation of McNabb is filtered through relief and joy that a black person is a quarterback for a professional football team."

McWhorter then took up the issue of affirmative action, which he says "has tended to crudely use skin color alone as a proxy for disadvantage." While McWhorter said that Limbaugh's view is hardly "unassailable," and pointed out that we have scarcely moved past race, it "hardly condemns [Limbaugh] as a benighted bigot."

It is interesting that both McWhorter and Jackson reduced the entire controversy to their own views of affirmative action: Jackson a staunch defender, and McWhorter a great deal more ambivalent and skeptical about it. The irony is that if there is one area in American life where the issue of racial preference or affirmative action did not compromise the presence of blacks it was sports. There might have been an affirmative action issue involving the hiring of more blacks for coaching and front-office jobs in sports, but there was never any question about special consideration on the field. If there was one area where blacks were able to compete with whites without question, it was sports. There was never any question about merit in sports, because it was supposed to be a pure competition, driven by the bottom line of the final score. The men and women who played were the best that were available. They served no intentional symbolic social purpose. It has always been the belief and the hope of many that sports could be divorced politically and socially from the society that brings it into being, a view that itself is culturally driven. Sports in this way did not represent social neutrality as much as it represented a kind of social objectivity. But this belies the fact that sports have always been seen by followers around the world as possessing political and social significance that, in fact, made sports highly appealing and dramatic. Who plays high-level sports has as much meaning as how well he or she plays. And so even in this arena of pure merit creeps the specter of racial preference. Were whites given racial preference before in how the position was defined to support white supremacy, or are blacks being given preference now in the cheerleading for them to succeed at it to prove that they are as good as whites?

Both Jackson and McWhorter are correct in seeing Limbaugh's comments as an attack on affirmative action. It is particularly sensitive because the quarterback position is so controversial; after all, NFL clubs administer Wonderlic, a short IQ test to draft-eligible players. Clearly at least some of the coaches are seeking a certain level of intelligence for certain positions. Blacks have denounced IQ tests almost since their inception as being unreliable as predictors and racially and culturally biased, as, in essence, forms of institutionalized racism. How much weight coaches and general managers give Wonderlic is unclear, but they must expect the test to tell them something about the players, otherwise why give it at all? One of the great battles in affirmative action is over job testing for employment and especially promotion, because African Americans tend to do poorer on such tests than whites. As mentioned earlier, blacks were supposedly unable to play quarterback because they were not intelligent enough to master the plays; IQ testing in football thus underscores a number of social and historical issues surrounding testing, the nature of intelligence, and black academic underachievement. (Blacks are the bottom demographic on virtually all IQ, achievement, and academic testing in the United States today, so if only motivated by pride or shame, then it is not surprising that they despise testing and constantly seek ways to discredit it.) Of course white quarterbacks like Vinny Testeverde and Terry Bradshaw who were not considered very bright and who had difficulty mastering playbooks, still had lengthy NFL careers. What does it mean that so many black quarterbacks are scramblers or seem to be to the public?

It should be noted that in 2005 J. Wyatt Monde-sire, the head of the Philadelphia chapter of the NAACP, wrote an opinion piece in his newspaper *The Philadelphia Sun* condemning McNabb for the terrible year he was having, in part caused by his sports hernia. McNabb, in fact, would have surgery in November before the season ended. Monde-sire wrote:

> However, this week I felt compelled to offer some personal thoughts about your horrific on-field performances this season because at their core, there is a lie you have tried to use to hide the fact that in reality you actually are not that good. In essence Donny, you are mediocre at best. And trying to disguise that fact behind some con-cocted reasoning that African American quarter-backs who can scramble and who can run the ball are somehow lesser field generals than one who can summon up dead-on passes at a whim is more insulting off the field than on.
>
> Your athleticism and unpredictability to sometimes run with the ball earlier in your career not only confused defenses, it also thrilled Eagles fans. At last, said many of us, now we have a multifaceted offensive threat whose talents threaten to not just dominate the NFC East Division, but

maybe the whole NFL for several years. We were elated. We were in awe. . . .

So, for you to continue to deny we fans (as well as yourself) one of the strongest elements of your game by claiming that "everybody expects black quarterbacks to scramble" not only amounts to a breach of faith but also belittles the real struggles of black athletes who've had to overcome real racial stereotypecasting in addition to downright segregation.[24]

In effect, Mondesire harshly criticized McNabb for lacking racial pride for wanting not to be stigmatized as a black quarterback. The sportswriters who chose to acknowledge this, particularly most white sportswriters, condemned Mondesire's column, but Mondesire was not writing the column for them but, rather, for his black readers, many of whom may have been more sympathetic to his views and who certainly may have felt that their claim on McNabb as a sports hero was different than that of whites. McNabb's response was, "I always thought the NAACP supported African Americans and didn't talk bad about them."[25]

Scrambling is not, as Jesse Jackson asserted, an innovation. After all, Fran Tarkenton, a white quarterback who played with Minnesota and New York for eighteen years, was known as the prototypical scrambler. Roger Staubach was a running quarterback, as was John Elway, another white quarterback, in the early days of his career. Steve Young was another scrambling quarterback. All of them are in the NFL Hall of Fame. But did running make these quarterbacks great, or was it, in the end, their passing and their general knowledge on the field? Scrambling is exciting to watch, but does a team actually win more with a scrambling quarterback? Consider this fact: in comparing Donovan McNabb with his peers after the 2009 season, McNabb had a lower career completion rate than did Brett Favre, Peyton Manning, Tom Brady, and Ben Roethlisberger, and all of those quarterbacks had won Super Bowls—McNabb had not. (On the other hand, McNabb has a higher career completion rate than three of the Eagles' legendary quarterbacks, Norm Van Brocklin, Sonny Jurgensen, and Ron Jaworski. It also is higher than Bart Starr's and Johnny Unitas's.)

There are good reasons many coaches, even in this day of the running quarterback, would prefer quarterbacks to not scramble. First, they are more apt to get hurt by taking more hits than they should. Second, they are likely to throw the ball better by not running. To ensure accuracy in throwing an object at a target, it is better if either the thrower or the target is stationary. The fact that black quarterbacks run a great deal and seem to make up plays on the fly may, in some instances, be more an indication of the lack of training that they receive in high school and college than anything else. Everyone, coaches and players, may be thinking that these athletes can simply get by on their vaunted "athleticism." They make up plays on the spot as if they were playing in the schoolyard. This has become the black style in football—something equivalent to playground basketball, so a black quarterback who runs is simply doing what is expected of him. Staid white quarterbacks without rhythm stay in the pocket; black quarterbacks with their crazy rhythm create jazz improvisation on the field. It sounds nice metaphorically for a black person or a white leftist to hear, but things are not quite that simple. Some may also see it as the inability of blacks to play the position in an orthodox manner; they make up in "athleticism" what they lack in intelligence. African Americans in this regard are what Hitler called them during the 1936 "Nazi" Olympics in Berlin, America's "Black Auxiliary," the uncouth naturals who can be taught to play games.

Jackson's point about how difficult it was in the past for blacks to play this position in the NFL is certainly true. It was extremely difficult in the 1970s and well into the 1980s. But since the University of Houston's Andre Ware, the first black quarterback to win the Heisman Trophy, was drafted in the first round of the 1990 draft, interest in black quarterbacks has escalated dramatically. And since the 1990s has there not been a real interest in some sportswriters to see black quarterbacks succeed in the pro ranks as circumstances have permitted to make the black quarterback a cause of sorts? Certainly no one can say that blacks must perform at a superhuman level these days to keep the position: Kordell Stewart, Jeff Blake, and Tony Banks were mediocre black quarterbacks who managed to stay in the NFL and who were starters for most of their careers. Is this an affirmative action effect, a racial preference? Almost certainly not—these men were probably the best options that the teams they played for had. But it is possible for conservatives to see it differently.

Jackson is right that Limbaugh used affirmative action as a slur or a smear. All conservatives do, and they have been effective with this strategy, but it would not have succeeded nearly as well had not some blacks themselves felt to some degree that affirmative action stigmatized them as a maimed, victimized people in constant need of encouragement and compensatory aid. Affirmative action might be making up for a past of unfairness and mistreatment, but who really wants to be the poster child for deprivation and a past burdened with insult and injury? That fact cannot be escaped if we are to understand the strength and weakness of affirmative action as a social policy of repair and restitution. Jackson wrote in his piece: "Once African Americans or Latinos or women are allowed to compete, they do just fine."[26] But this is terribly simplistic and does not address the fundamental question of the nature of the competition or the epistemology of competition itself, both of which are lines of attacks by leftists such as Jackson when it is convenient for them to do so, and not without reason. Everything is not "just fine" when people are "allowed" to compete. For advocates of affirmation action, the policy itself is of limited utility in just allowing people to compete (this is merely the early cold war, Jackie Robinson model of liberalism as an ideological mechanism for color-blind arbitration); there must be assurances that some will succeed, which is why affirmative action came into existence, for what the advocates of affirmative action desire most, and this seems sensible if one accepts that the rewards of a society are not distributed accidentally or fairly, is a result that would have been obtained if racism had never existed. Since no one knows what that result would have been, one can only push for the maximum number that can possibly be achieved, which is why affirmative action, as a spoils game, does not ever produce satisfaction but simply breeds a psychic and political restlessness and a demand for more. Jackson's last point about Limbaugh's obsession with the liberal media is well taken in that Limbaugh himself is proof that conservatives certainly have access to the airwaves and to the print media. It also is true, as many liberals have pointed out, that no one as to the left as Limbaugh is to the right is on the air. (The Right would probably reply, in *Jeopardy*-like fashion, "What is NPR, if not the liberals' answer to right-wing radio?") This is not Limbaugh's fault or doing: conservative viewpoints sell better in the open market of radio programming than do liberal viewpoints. The Left had better learn to sell itself better to its own constituency, or perhaps the format simply does not suit how the Left wishes to get affirmation of its opinions. Moreover, the liberal view has its outlets, powerful ones, as Jackson himself is aware, from certain private foundations, Rockefeller, MacArthur, and Mellon, to universities and their presses, to many important newspapers such as the *New York Times*, the *Washington Post*, and the *Los Angeles Times*. But the conservatives have been very effective; otherwise, how does one explain Limbaugh's ability, as well as that of Ann Coulter, Sean Hannity, Mark Steyn, and others of that persuasion, to be such a prominent figure in the public discourse? Right-wing pundits may be correct in saying that many of their opinions get distorted or ridiculed in the liberal mainstream, but they are not ignored.

McWhorter's skepticism about affirmative action colors his remarks. He claims that Limbaugh's remark about McNabb being overrated because of the color of his skin is not racist in the least. Yet it is difficult to see how one can be so sure of that. Why is it not reasonable to think that Limbaugh thinks that blacks are not capable of being quarterbacks because of their race, and that white liberal journalists and a liberal NFL establishment prop them up as something good for the country? One cannot say for sure that Limbaugh means that, but one also cannot say for sure that he does not. What if Limbaugh were to say about a noted black doctor or scientist or, heaven forbid, a black public intellectual or scholar, such as, say, Cornel West or Henry Louis Gates, that he has the reputation he has because whites have created that reputation for political reasons, because we as a society need public examples of brainy black people or black people who can reasonably pass as brainy? Placing the comment in a different context might illuminate it a bit differently. And this, of course, has been said about certain black intellectuals. Indeed, historically, it has been said about blacks in every place that blacks have appeared where they were not expected.

Coda: The King of Wishful Thinking

In May 2009 Limbaugh joined an effort by Dave Checketts, the former president of the New York Knicks and founder of Sports Capital Partners Worldwide, which owns the St. Louis Blues hockey team, to buy the St. Louis Rams, a franchise that has faltered in recent years and was made available by the death in 2008 of owner Georgia Frontiere. For Limbaugh this was, at last, his entry into the upper-crust world of men who owned NFL franchises, "the men he thought of as friends, rich men like himself whose owners' boxes he had shared over the years."[27]

These men did nothing to help Limbaugh when protests erupted once the news leaked out about his partnership with Checketts. In fact Indianapolis Colts owner Jim Irsay publicly opposed Limbaugh: "I, myself, couldn't even consider voting for him," Irsay said at a meeting of NFL owners. "When there are comments that have been made that are inappropriate, incendiary and insensitive . . . our words do damage, and it's something that we don't need."[28] Jesse Jackson and Al Sharpton, whom Limbaugh had satirized for years as the "Justice Brothers," race hustlers scamming guilt-ridden whites, pressured NFL Commissioner Roger Goodell. DeMaurice Smith, the head of the NFL Players Association, also denounced the idea of Limbaugh as a potential owner. Even some African American players said that they would not play for a team if Limbaugh was one of the owners.

Several factors conspired against Limbaugh, not simply that he was a conservative (probably several NFL owners are politically conservative) but that he was a sort of agent provocateur, which actually disqualified him to enter the conservative *industry* of pro football. First, not only what Limbaugh said about McNabb in 2003 but other remarks about blacks, many of which were fabricated by his enemies, were brought to light, forcing Limbaugh into a state of denial, an untenable position for a controversial public figure. To be sure some of the worst statements Limbaugh never said. And some of his statements, such as calling Barack Obama "the Magic Negro," which he took from a piece in the *Los Angeles Times*, were legitimate, even brilliant, political satire. But his insistence on calling Obama "a man child" and his emphasis on Obama being "unqualified" and "inexperienced" seem a not-so-subtle bit of racial red-meat tossing for his audience, many of whom think they are saddled with an affirmative action president. Ironically it was the entertainment aspect of his show (Limbaugh purposely tries to bait people at times) that ultimately cost him, twice, being able to enter the world of pro football, one of America's great entertainments. To his credit, Limbaugh's chief of staff is an African American who goes by the nom de guerre Bo Snerdley, and one of the regular guest hosts for his program is African American economist Walter Williams. In this regard, as Limbaugh has rightly pointed out, his show is more integrated than some network and cable political commentary programs. (Limbaugh has been a longtime friend and defender of Supreme Court Justice Clarence Thomas and also counts Muhammad Ali as one of his heroes.) Second, the fact that Obama was elected president made it impossible to have an owner in a league dominated by blacks who so emphatically wished that Obama would fail. Had a liberal white been elected president and Limbaugh had said the same, it would be less of an explosive issue. Third, the NFL's image problem has steadily elevated Donovan McNabb since 2003. Consider these high-profile cases involving African American football players: Michael Vick's highly publicized conviction for dog fighting in 2007, Ray Lewis's trial for murder in 2000 (he was acquitted), Plaxico Burress's accidental self-inflicted gun wound and subsequent conviction on a weapons charge in 2008, Rae Carruth's 2001 conviction for murdering his pregnant girlfriend, the criminal career of Adam "Pacman" Jones, who was serially arrested between 2005 and 2008 and suspended several times, and Tank Johnson's various arrests in 2005 and 2006. As the NFL struggles to deal with its wayward players and the image that it is a "gangsta" league full of inner-city thugs, McNabb has emerged as one of the most respectable and respected men in pro football. Nothing demonstrated this more than the Eagles' signing of Vick when he was released from prison. What could help Vick's damaged reputation more than being associated with McNabb as his understudy, as the man who would get Vick on the right track? Whether it was all simply public relations or whether there was some substance beneath this is not really the issue: the point is that the Eagles and the NFL itself thought McNabb's image was helpful in reinstating Vick. (Interestingly, in his conflict with wide receiver Terrell Owens during the 2005 and 2006 seasons, which resulted ultimately in the Eagles suspending Owens when he became a disruptive force in demanding more money, the press and the public clearly sided with McNabb, but McNabb's black teammates were much more sympathetic to Owens, thinking McNabb a "company man.") McNabb's standing as the leading African American citizen of pro football was underscored most recently by the allegations of sexual misbehavior in 2009 and 2010 against white Pittsburgh Steelers quarterback Ben Roethlisberger. A man whose image had become this important, an important face, black face, for the league itself, would not take very well the idea of someone like Limbaugh being considered for ownership. In the end, the league owners decided that McNabb was far more vital to their survival, their legitimacy as an American institution in the twenty-first century, than Limbaugh could ever be. The league was about to be associated with vocal opposition to both diversity and affirmative action. And so the decision as to who would be left twisting in the wind when the public learned of the Checketts partnership was, colloquially put, a no-brainer. Let the fat man swing.

PART II

Heroism and the Republic of Sports

4

American Integration, Black Heroism, and the Meaning of Jackie Robinson

The sun is very important. The theory, practice, and spectacle of bullfighting have all been built on the assumption of the presence of the sun and when it does not shine, over a third of the bullfight is missing. [Without] the sun the best bullfighter is not there. He is like a man without a shadow.

— Ernest Hemingway,
Death in the Afternoon

BY THE END of our semicentennial celebration of Jackie Robinson's breaking the color line in professional baseball, the sheer volume of repetitious, melodramatic acclaim for his valor is likely to make him seem more trite than titanic. But there is something vital to be learned about the nature of American society and American race relations by trying to understand just what the heroism of this man is supposed to mean, especially to blacks today, for Robinson's achievement was fraught from the beginning with ambivalence, both his own and that of the blacks for whom he was a hero. And that ambivalence is characteristic of black assimilation into many arenas of American life.

Robinson arguably was the person who launched the American era of racial integration after World War II. This rush and flood of people and events—the *Brown* decision, the Montgomery bus boycott, the sit-ins, the March on Washington, Birmingham and Selma, Martin Luther King Jr., the Watts riots, Malcolm X, affirmative action, multiculturalism, the Million Man March—provoked unprecedented historical change in how Americans perceived pluralism and race, but shockingly, in the end, did not at all lessen the abiding sense of alienation that African Americans felt toward their native land.

A famous passage in Richard Wright's *Black Boy* discusses this alienation: Wright describes "the essential bleakness of black life in America" and says that blacks have "never been allowed to catch the full spirit of Western civilization." Agreeing with Wright, Ralph Ellison later said that "Western culture must be won, confronted like the animal in a Spanish bullfight, dominated by the red shawl of codified experience and brought heaving to its knees." The sports metaphor, or perhaps more precisely the metaphor of spectacle, is crucial in explaining the complexity of Jackie Robinson's significance as a race hero. The metaphor suggests a kind of black masculine spin on the Hemingwayesque moral code of grace under pressure: a combination of stoicism and élan, of the tragic and triumphant confrontation with an adversarial, savage universe.

What Ellison values here is a style of action, a principle of engagement, that evoked what his disciple, Albert Murray, was to call "the blues hero." Ellison's metaphor suggests that African Americans must claim Western culture through an act not of submission but of domination, through the power of ordering their experience, sculpting it out of both the chaos of life and the dominant, inimical white culture. Western culture is, thus, a complex set of brute impulses and vested interests represented in various institutions, a force that one must make one's own by courageously making demands of it.

Jackie Robinson was, most profoundly, an Ellisonian blues hero. He confronted Western experience publicly and alone, yet within the democratic context of a team. He also confronted both absurdity and injustice, taking his chances within the sunlit arena (baseball was still, like the bullfight, performed most often in the afternoon), armed solely with a set of highly specialized, elite skills. Robinson became a public spectacle in a way that no other African American had quite been before, and he subdued Western culture through his sheer will to win.

It is telling that we did not celebrate with anything near the same intensity the semicentennial of Joe Louis's 1938 defeat of the German Max Schmeling, in its time an athletic event of at least as much political importance as Robinson's integration of baseball. Nor was the anniversary of Jesse Owens's track victories at the 1936 Berlin Olympics—also considered a momentous event in race relations—met with as much fanfare. Both earlier events were public spectacles in which blacks seized an Ellisonian moment of domination. Indeed, both events might be said to be even more important than Robinson's entry into the big leagues because of their international significance. Yet it is probably, in some measure, their international significance that contributes to our valuing them less than we should, our American provincialism being what it is.

Robinson's greater resonance as a hero has to do with the very local meaning of baseball, not merely as a sport but as a well-ordered ritual of American life associated with contradictory impulses that grew out of its Industrial Age origins: an obsession with quantification and statistics and a nostalgic quest for pastoralism.

Gunnar Myrdal's *An American Dilemma*, published just three years before Robinson's ascension to the major leagues, presented a mountain of numbers and graphs demonstrating the disorder of black American life, as did, of course, any number of sociological studies done over the years, by both black and white scholars. And at that time the dominant portrayals of black Americans included such degrading pastoral images as Sambo, the comic darky, Old Black Joe, and other variations of minstrelsy. What more vivid, extraordinary way was there for blacks to reinvent and regenerate themselves than through the very cultural means that had been used to deny their humanity, through the pastoralism and statistics of baseball?

Baseball is also tied to our mystical, sentimental idea of democracy as teamwork and fair play. That is why Robinson's act of assimilation-as-heroism has had such a powerful impact on the American imagination; it is also what has made it so tangled and, for many blacks, so paradoxical, for blacks always approached professional baseball, from the time they were denied the opportunity to play it alongside whites in the 1880s, as a vehicle for assimilation.

Arising out of the insult and stigma of segregation, the Negro leagues were never meant to be ends in themselves. But because through the leagues blacks developed a more elaborate and enduring institutional relationship with baseball than with any other sport, baseball became not only a means for assimilation but also a black cultural and commercial venture. Black baseball demonstrated black independence as much as it showed whites that blacks were able and competitive and desired very much to play baseball with them.

By expressing the desire for freedom and respect, even esteem, through entrepreneurship and enterprise, as well as by demonstrating the nationalistic urge of blacks to act independently of whites, the leagues—such as black colleges, black churches, and other "shadow" institutions that blacks developed— became ends in themselves, taking on a compelling racial *mission*. Robinson's heroism, as a contradictory form of liberation, cannot be understood outside of this conundrum, one that explains a great deal about the ambivalence that African Americans have felt about integration as a political and social goal.

This ambivalence among blacks is evident in a debate that took place in the press between Robinson and Effa Manley, co-owner with her husband Abe, of the premier Negro league team, the Newark Eagles. In June 1948, one year after Robinson's major league debut and amidst the general sense among both blacks and whites that integrated professional baseball was here to stay. Robinson published an article in *Ebony* titled "What's Wrong with Negro Baseball?" In it he described Negro league baseball as being chaotic and mediocre. He never had a contract with the Kansas City Monarchs, the Negro league team he played for in 1945. According to Robinson, the umpiring was sloppy and often biased; there was virtually no spring training or conditioning for the players; the pay was too low; the bus travel was interminable and uncomfortable; there was too much barnstorming; and road accommodations were awful.

Robinson wrote that when he first joined a Brooklyn Dodger farm club, "I was convinced that my leaving Negro baseball would stimulate interest in the colored leagues. Later it was my earnest desire to do all I could to make good with the Dodgers because I felt it would make the fellows in the [Negro] league I just left play harder, train harder, and give the fans much better baseball."

Two months later the sharp-tongued Manley answered Robinson in an article titled "Negro Baseball Isn't Dead!" in another black publication called *Our World.* She argued that Negro league pay was on a par with that in the white leagues, especially when one considered that the Negro teams drew fewer fans than white teams and thus generated less revenue for their owners. Indeed, she argued, it was Robinson, the gate attraction for the Brooklyn Dodgers, who was being underpaid in the major leagues. She maintained that bus travel was comfortable, better than going by train, and that road accommodations were bad because of Jim Crow, not because of the venality of Negro league owners.

She reminded Robinson that at least her Newark Eagles, if not other Negro league teams, had contractual arrangements with their players, which major league owners refused to honor, and that the barnstorming was necessary largely because Negro leagues lacked their own playing facilities. "Wittingly or unwittingly," she wrote, "Jackie Robinson has lent his powerful name to the destruction of Negro baseball."

Here, in miniature, is the black debate over integration as both a tactic and a principle—or, more precisely, the black debate over the meaning of pluralism in American life. Robinson's description of Negro league baseball is accurate but also self-serving, as it justifies major league owners' use of black baseball as a virtual labor pool, a practice that gutted the Negro leagues.

What Robinson described was so chaotic that Negro baseball could hardly deserve respect as a business or even as something organized. (White professional baseball, both major and minor leagues, always called itself "organized," suggesting that all other professional baseball was disorganized.) Robinson was under no obligation to say anything at all about his Negro league experience to explain his desire to play in the major leagues. He must have denounced it in such harsh terms to justify, to himself and to other blacks, his own decision to abandon black baseball.

Effa Manley's view was also accurate, as well as self-serving. Although many of the problems in the Negro leagues were a direct result of racism, Manley here, as well as in other pieces she wrote and press interviews she gave, said the Negro league owners' lack of unity greatly exacerbated their disorganization. She seemed to be making a pitch for racial loyalty, virtually admitting that her team and Negro baseball existed because whites refused to use black players.

The owners of many black businesses, in fact, opposed integration on the grounds that it would break up the virtual monopoly they enjoyed. Black professionals—doctors, lawyers, architects, and the like—could hardly expect to have clients and patients, especially in a culture that so promoted white supremacy, without appealing to racial loyalty. In short, for Manley, what made racism so difficult for blacks was their inability to generate an organized, unified response to it. But basing commerce on racial loyalty suggests that blacks have no basis for community beyond the forces of segregation and racism that have made them a "community" in the first place.

Both Robinson and Manley were responding from their positions as members of other "communities" as well: Robinson endorsed a kind of individualism because he was, after all, a worker for hire. Manley, on the other hand, supported group organization and group integrity because she was an employer who was losing her workers to a competitor. Both, however, represented the rise of a highly driven, urban black middle class, essential to the development of a truly democratic black community and true democratic participation by blacks in the larger society.

Was pluralism for blacks in America to mean the redemption of the group through the actions of the individual, or the redemption of the group through the group itself? Was power in America diffused in a muddled middle, where remarkable individuals therefore made a difference, or was power largely the function and expression of a group dynamic and cohesion? In this instance, in 1948, Robinson was the radical who challenged the system, while Manley was the reactionary who wanted things to remain the same. But also in this instance a powerful public drama was being enacted and a powerful public debate was taking place about the nature and meaning of the African American social contract.

What did integration cost? I have never heard a black person mention Jackie Robinson without noting that he died a physical wreck, at the age of fifty-three—a fact attributed to the stress of his years as a major league player. And it is undeniable that once the Negro leagues died, once baseball ceased to have an institutional presence in black life, blacks generally lost interest in professional baseball as spectators and fans.

What makes Robinson such a fascinating figure is how—as a symbol of integration—he combined militance with a sense of martyrdom and combined defiance and deference. We have the 1944 Robinson who was court-martialed for insubordination to his white officers. We have the 1949 Robinson who testified before the House Un-American Activities Committee (HUAC) at its request to reassure whites of black patriotism after Paul Robeson said that blacks ought not to fight for the United States against the Soviet Union. (The irony of asking a man who could not stand being in a Jim Crow army to testify as an example of blacks' loyalty and willingness to serve their country seems to have escaped the members of the HUAC.) We have the Robinson who endured three years of abuse as a major leaguer, instructed by Dodger executive Branch Rickey not to fight back. And we have the Robinson who, later, took umbrage at even the smallest slight and argued about anything he did not like on the field of play.

Robinson was both Mr. Inside and Mr. Outside—
he reassured white authority, but his very presence
seemed to undermine it. He espoused a belief in
democratic ideals, but the singularity of his presence and the reaction to it revealed how far Americans were from achieving those ideals. In this way
he was much like Martin Luther King Jr., who also
was Mr. Inside and Mr. Outside, reassuring whites
that he supported their values while both intention-
ally and inadvertently subverting them.

The ambiguity of Jackie Robinson's heroism
takes on another dimension today, given the cultural
significance of black athletes in contemporary
America. John Hoberman takes up this issue in his
book *Darwin's Athletes*. He intimates that blacks,
for reasons not all of their own making, are too psychologically invested in their athletes, generally
having much less respect or appreciation for, say,
intellectual life and achievement.

It seems true that the harsh oppression that
blacks have endured, which often created an intense need to conform to the group to achieve unity
and gain protection—coupled with the rampant
anti-intellectualism in American life generally—
caused blacks to overvalue their physical accomplishments. But athletes often best represent the

heroism and achievement of an oppressed group, because their accomplishments are not seen as compromised by the fact that the athletes may be paid for their efforts. This is especially true among blacks because of their continuing concern that black masculinity be seen as an uncompromised, assertive political and cultural force. In our patriarchal culture, black freedom has historically been the quest for black manhood.

Intellectual achievement, on the other hand, long has been suspect. African Americans historically have not been able to reward their best intellectuals and thus could never fully trust those who were largely supported by whites.

Moreover, as male intellectuals seem compromised, they appear decidedly less manly, especially to an oppressed group that devoutly wishes to see the arrogance of its oppressors challenged. And even as blacks may prize their engineers, scientists, and researchers, intellectuals do not operate in a framework where their besting of white competitors is the public spectacle that it is for the professional or highly placed amateur athlete. Although blacks have never been able to consistently support or reward their best athletes either, the athletes' excellence, and the political and cultural significance of that excellence for the group as a whole, is largely unaffected by that fact. Robinson was an outstanding ballplayer in the Negro leagues, and he was an outstanding player in the major leagues.

Hoberman, viewing American professional sports as an arena controlled by whites, argues that it is a sign of blacks' political and cultural weakness that athletes have become such a potent representation of who and what they are and such a crucial expression of their cultural assertion. This is true. But it is also true that what blacks may be responding to in black athleticism is a form of the American pioneer myth of reinvention and discovery—the need to conquer a wilderness that demands sheer physical courage. This mythology speaks to the tragedy of race, relying as it does on the need for human struggle to transcend race.

Is it possible that there can be, in the sunlit arena where one confronts the animal of Western culture, a man without a shadow? Can a black hero be without the shadow of race, the shadow of ambivalence about assimilation? Is the African American condemned, as the lyrics of the old song "Me and My Shadow" suggest, to prove his or her humanity simply by imitating whites?

This is what we are forced to ask about the achievement of every great and important black athlete, and every black person whose achievements require the compromise of assimilation. In remembering Jackie Robinson, what we have is a poignant rendering of a glorious fanfare of uncertain trumpets.

5

Performance and Reality:
Race, Sports, and the Modern World

THE CELEBRATION of the fiftieth anniversary of Jackie Robinson's breaking the color line in major league baseball was one of the most pronounced and prolonged ever held in the history of our Republic in memory of a black man or of an athlete. It seems nearly obvious that, on one level, our preoccupation was not so much with Robinson himself—previous milestone anniversaries of his starting at first base for the Brooklyn Dodgers in April 1947 produced little fanfare—as it was with ourselves and our own dilemma about race, a problem that strikes us simultaneously as being intractable and "progressing" toward resolution, as a chronic, inevitably fatal disease and as a test of national character that we will, finally, pass.

Robinson was the man white society could not defeat in the short term, though his untimely death at age fifty-three convinced many that the stress of the battle defeated him in the long run. In this respect Robinson did become something of an uneasy elegiac symbol of race relations, satisfying everyone's psychic needs: blacks, with a redemptive black hero who did not sell out and in whose personal tragedy was a corporate triumph over racism, and whites, with a black hero who showed assimilation to be a triumphant act. For each group it was important that Robinson was a hero for the other. All of this was easier to accomplish because Robinson played baseball, a "pastoral" sport of innocence and triumphalism in the American mind, a sport of epic romanticism, a sport whose golden age is always associated with childhood. In the end Robinson as tragic hero represented, paradoxically, depending on the faction, how far we have come and how much more needs to be done.

As a nation I think we needed the evocation of Robinson to save us from the nihilistic fires of race: from the trials of O. J. Simpson (the failed black athletic hero who seems nothing more than a symbol of self-centered consumption); from the Rodney King trial and subsequent riot in Los Angeles; and, most significant, from the turmoil over affirmative action, an issue not only about *how* blacks are to achieve a place in American society but about the perennial existential question: *Can* black people have a rightful place of dignity in this society, or is the stigma of race to taint everything they do and desire? We know that some of the most admired celebrities in the United States today—in many instances, excessively so by some whites—are black athletes. Michael Jordan, one of the most admired athletes in modern history, was the face of a $10 billion industry, and beloved all over the world. But what did Jordan want except what most insecure, upwardly bound Americans want? More of what he already had to assure himself that he did, indeed, have what he wanted. Jordan was not simply a brilliant athlete, the personification of an unstoppable will but, like all figures in popular culture, a complex, charismatic representation of desire, his own and ours.

Perhaps we reached back for Robinson (just as we reached back for an ailing Muhammad Ali, the boastful athlete as expiatory dissident, at the Olympics) because of our need for an athlete to transcend his self-absorbed prowess and quest for championships, or whose self-absorption and quest for titles meant something deeper politically and socially, told us something a bit more important about ourselves as a racially divided, racially stricken nation. A baseball strike during the period 1994–1995, which canceled the World Series, gambling scandals in college basketball, ceaseless recruiting violations with student athletes, rape and drug cases involving athletes, the increasing commercialization of sports resulting in more tax concessions to team owners and ever-more-expensive stadiums, the wild inflation of salaries, prize money and endorsement fees for the most elite athletes—all of this led to a general dissatisfaction with sports, or at least to some legitimate uneasiness about them, as many people see sports, both amateur and professional, more and more as a depraved enterprise, as a Babylon of greed, dishonesty, and hypocrisy, or as an industry out to rob the public blind. At what better moment to resurrect Robinson, a man who played for the competition and the glory, for the love of the game and the honor of his profession, and as a tribute to the dignity and pride of his race in what many of us perceive, wrongly, to have been a simpler, less commercial time?

What, indeed, is the place of black people in our realm? Perhaps, at this point in history, we are all, black and white, as mystified by that question as we were at the end of the Civil War when faced with the prospect that the slave and the free must live together as equal citizens, or must try to. The question has always signified that affirmative action—a public policy for the unconditional inclusion of the African American that has existed, with all of its good and failed intentions, in the air of American racial reform since black people were officially freed, even, indeed, in the age of abolition with voices such as Lydia Maria Child's and Frederick Douglass's—is about the making of an African into an American and the meaning of that act for our democracy's ability to absorb all. We were struck by Robinson's story because it was as profound, as mythic, as any European immigrant's story about how Americans are made. We Americans seem to have blundered about in our history with two clumsy contrivances strapped to our backs, unreconciled and weighty: our democratic traditions and race. What makes Robinson so significant is that he seemed to have found a way to balance this baggage in the place that is so much the stuff of our dreams: the level playing field of top-flight competitive athletics. "Athletics," stated Robinson in his first autobiography, *Jackie Robinson: My Own Story* (ghostwritten by black sportswriter Wendell Smith), "both school and professional, come nearer to offering an American Negro equality of opportunity than does any other field of social and economic activity." It is not so much that this is true as that Robinson believed it, and that most Americans today, black and white, still do or still want to. This is one of the important aspects of modern sports in a democratic society that has saved us from being totally cynical about them. Sports are the ultimate meritocracy. Might it be said that sports are what all other professional activities and business endeavors, all leisure pursuits and hobbies, in our society aspire to be?

If nothing else, Robinson, an unambiguous athletic hero for both races and a symbol of sacrifice on the altar of racism, is our most magnificent case of affirmative action. He entered a lily-white industry amidst cries that he was unqualified (not entirely unjustified, as Robinson had had only one year of professional experience in the Negro leagues, although, on the other hand, he was one of the most gifted athletes of his generation), and he succeeded, *on merit*, beyond anyone's wildest hope. And here the sports metaphor is a perfectly literal expression of the traditional democratic belief of that day: If given the chance, anyone can make it on his ability, with no remedial aid or special compensation, on a level playing field. Here was the fulfillment of our American Creed, to use Gunnar Myrdal's term (*An American Dilemma* had appeared only a year before Robinson was signed by the Dodgers), of fair play and equal opportunity. Here was our democratic orthodoxy of color-blind competition realized. Here was an instance where neither the principle nor its application could be impugned. Robinson was proof, just as heavyweight champion Joe Louis and Olympic track star Jesse Owens were during the Great Depression, that sports helped vanquish the stigma of race.

In this instance sports are extraordinarily useful because their values can endorse any political ideology. It must be remembered that the British had used sports—and modern sports are virtually their invention—as a colonial and missionary tool, not always with evil intentions but almost always with hegemonic ones. Sports had also been used by their subjects as a tool of liberation, as anti-hegemonic, as they learned to beat the British at their own games. "To win was to be human," said African scholar Manthia Diawara, and for the colonized and the oppressed, sports meant just that, in the same way that for the British to win was to be British. Sports

were meant to preserve and symbolize the hegemony of the colonizer, even as they inspired the rev-
olutionary spirit of the oppressed. Sports have been
revered by fascists and communists, by free market-
ers and filibusters. They have also been, paradoxically, reviled by all of those political factions. Sports
may be among the most powerful human expressions in all of history. Why, then, could sports not
serve the United States ideologically in whatever
way people decided to define democratic values
during this, the American Century, when we became the most powerful purveyors of sports in all
history?

Both the Left and the Right have used Robinson
for their own ends. The Left, suspicious of popular
culture as a set of cheap commercial distractions
constructed by the ruling class of post-industrial society to delude the masses, saw Robinson as a racial
martyr, a working-class member of an oppressed minority who challenged the white hegemony as symbolized by sports as a political reification of superior, privileged expertise; the Right, suspicious of
popular culture as an expression of the rule of the
infantile taste of the masses, saw him as a challenge
to the idea of restricting talent pools and restricting
markets to serve a dubious privilege. For the con-

servative today, Robinson is the *classic, fixed* example of affirmative action properly applied as the extension of opportunity to all, regardless of race, class, gender, or outcome. For the liberal, Robinson is an example of the *process* of affirmative action as the erosion of white male hegemony, where outcome is the very point of the exercise—affirmative action is about the redistribution of power. For the conservative, it is about releasing deserving talent. This seems little more than the standard difference in views between the conservative and the liberal about the meaning of democratic values and social reform. For the conservative, the story of Robinson and affirmative action is about conformity: Robinson, as symbolic Negro, *joined* the mainstream. For the liberal, the story of Robinson and affirmative action is about resistance: Robinson, as symbolic Negro, *changed* the mainstream. The conservative does not want affirmative action to disturb what Lothrop Stoddard called "the iron law of inequality." The liberal wants affirmative action to create complete equality, as all inequality is structural and environmental. (Proof of how much Robinson figured in the affirmative action debate can be found in Steve Sailer's "How Jackie Robinson Desegregated America," a cover story in the April 8, 1996, *National Review,* and in Anthony Pratkanis and Marlene Turner's liberal article, "Nine Principles of Successful Affirmative Action: Mr. Branch Rickey, Mr. Jackie Robinson, and the Integration of Baseball," in the Fall 1994 issue of *Nine: A Journal of Baseball History and Social Policy Perspectives*.) Whoever may be right in this regard, it can be said that inasmuch as either side endorsed the idea, both sides were wrong about sports eliminating the stigma of race. Over the years since Robinson's arrival, sports have, in many respects, intensified race and racialist thinking or, more precisely, anxiety about race and racialist thinking.

Race is not merely a system of categorizations of privileged or discredited abilities but, rather, a system of conflicting abstractions about what it means to be human. Sports are not a material realization of the ideal that those who succeed deserve to succeed; they are a paradox of play as work, of highly competitive, highly pressurized work as a form of romanticized play, a system of rules and regulations governing both a real and a symbolic activity, and suggesting, in the stunning complexity of its performance, both conformity and revolt. Our mistake about race is assuming that it is largely an expres-

sion of irrationality when it is, in fact, to borrow
G. K. Chesterton's phrase, "nearly reasonable, but
not quite." Our mistake about sports is assuming
that they are largely minor consequences of our
two great American gifts: marketing and technology. Their pervasiveness and their image, their
evocation of desire and transcendence, are the result of marketing. Their elaborate modalities of
engineering—from the conditioning of the athletes
to the construction of the arenas to the fabrication
of the tools and machines that athletes use and
the apparel that they wear—are the result of our
technology. But modern sports, although extraordinary expressions of marketing and technology, are
far deeper, far more atavistic, than either. Perhaps
sports, in some ways, are as atavistic as race.

THE WHITENESS OF THE WHITE ATHLETE

In the December 8, 1997, *Sports Illustrated* article
"Whatever Happened to the White Athlete?" S. L.
Price wrote about the dominant presence of black
athletes in professional basketball (80 percent
black), professional football (67 percent black), and
track and field (93 percent of gold medalists are
black). He also argued that while African Americans

made up only 17 percent of major league baseball players, "[During] the past 25 years, blacks have been a disproportionate offensive force, winning 41 percent of the Most Valuable Player awards." (And the number of blacks in baseball does not include the black Latinos, for whom baseball is more popular than it is with American blacks.) Blacks also dominate boxing, a sport not dealt with in the article. Price wrote, "Whites have in some respects become sports' second-class citizens. In a surreal inversion of Robinson's era, white athletes are frequently the ones now tagged by the stereotypes of skin color." He concluded by suggesting that white sprinter Kevin Little, in competition, can feel "the slightest hint—and it is not more than a hint—of what Jackie Robinson felt 50 years ago." It is more than a little ludicrous to suggest that white athletes today even remotely, even as a hint, are experiencing something even similar to what Robinson experienced. White athletes, even when they play sports dominated by blacks, are still entering an industry not only controlled by whites in every phase of authority and operation but also largely sustained by white audiences. When Robinson departed the Negro leagues at the end of 1945, he left a sports structure that was largely regulated, managed, and patronized by blacks, inasmuch as blacks could ever, with the resources available to them in the 1920s, 1930s, and 1940s, profitably and proficiently run a sports league. Robinson's complaints about the Negro leagues—the incessant barnstorming, the bad accommodations, the poor umpiring, the inadequate spring training—were not only similar to white criticism of the Negro leagues but mirrored the criticism that blacks tended to levy against their own organizations and organizational skills. As Sol White made clear in his seminal 1907 *History of Colored Base Ball*, black people continued to play baseball after they were banned by white professional leagues to show to themselves and to the world that they were capable of *organizing* themselves into teams and leagues. When Robinson left the Kansas City Monarchs, he entered a completely white world, much like the world in which he operated as a star athlete at UCLA. It was, in part, because Robinson was used to the white world of sports from his college days that Branch Rickey selected him to become the first black man to play major league baseball. Today, when white athletes enter sports dominated by blacks, they do not enter a black *organization* but something akin to a mink-lined black ghetto. (My use of the word "ghetto" here is not meant to suggest anything about oppression, political or otherwise.) Although blacks dominate the most popular team sports, they still make up only 9 percent of all people in the United States who make a living or try to make a living as athletes, less than their percentage in the general population.

What I found most curious about Price's article is that he gave no plausible reason for blacks' domination of these particular sports. He quoted various informants to the effect that blacks must work harder than whites at sports. "Inner-city kids," William Ellerbee, basketball coach at Simon Gratz High in Philadelphia, said, "look at basketball as a matter of life or death." In a similar article in the *Washington Post* on the black makeup of the NBA, Jon Barry, a white player for the Atlanta Hawks, offered: "Maybe the suburban types or the white people have more things to do." Much of this is undoubtedly true. Traditionally, from the early days of professional baseball in the mid-nineteenth century and of professional boxing in Regency England, sports were seen by the men and boys of the poor and working classes as a way out of poverty, or at least out of the normally backbreaking, low-paying work that the poor male was offered. And certainly (though some black intellectuals may argue the point, feeling it suggests that black cultural life is impoverished) there probably is more to do or more available to amuse and enlighten in a middle-class suburb than in an inner-city neighborhood, even if the perception is that some whites who live in the suburbs are provincial and philistine.

Nonetheless, these explanations do not quite satisfy. Ultimately the discussion in both articles comes down to genetics. There is nothing wrong with thinking about genetic variations. After all, what does the difference in human beings mean, and what is its source? Still, if, for instance, Jewish people dominated football and basketball (as they once did boxing), would there be such a fixation to explain it genetically? The fact is, historically, blacks have been a genetic wonder, monstrosity, or aberration to whites, and they are still burdened by this implicit sense that they are not quite "normal." From the mid-nineteenth century—with its racist intellectuals like Samuel Cartwright (a Southern medical doctor whose use of minstrel-style jargon, "Dysesthaesia Ethiopica," to describe black people as having thick minds and insensitive bodies is similar to the talk of today's racist geneticists about "fast-twitch" muscles) and Samuel Morton (whose *Crania Americana* tried to classify races by skull size), as well as Louis Agassiz, Arthur de Gobineau, and Josiah Nott (who, with George Gliddon, produced the extremely popular *Types of Mankind* in 1854, which argued that races had been created as separate species)—to Charles Murray and Richard Herrnstein's defense of intelligence quotients to explain economic and status differences among racial and ethnic groups in *The Bell Curve* (1994), blacks have been subjected to a great deal of scientific or so-called scientific scrutiny, much of it misguided, if not outright malicious, and all of it to justify the political and economic hegemony of whites. For instance, Lothrop Stoddard, in *The Revolt against Civilization* (1922), a book nearly identical in some of its themes and polemics to *The Bell Curve*, created a being called the Under-Man, a barbarian unfit for civilization. (Perhaps this is why some black intellectuals loathe the term "underclass.") Stoddard wrote, "The rarity of mental as compared with physical superiority in the human species is seen on every hand. Existing savage and barbaric races of a demonstrably low average level of intelligence, like the negroes [*sic*], are physically vigorous, in fact, possess an animal vitality apparently greater than that of the intellectually higher races." There is no escaping the doctrine that for blacks to be physically superior biologically, they must be inferior intellectually and, thus, inferior as a group, Under-People.

But even if it were true that blacks were athletically superior to whites, why then would they not dominate all sports instead of just a handful? There might be a more plainly structural explanation for black dominance in certain sports. This is not to say that genes may have nothing to do with it, but only to say that, at this point, genetic arguments have been far from persuasive and, in their implications, more than a little pernicious.

It is easy enough to explain black dominance in boxing. It is the Western sport that has the longest history of black participation, so there is tradition. Moreover, it is a sport that has always attracted poor and marginalized men. Black men have persistently made up a disproportionate share of the poor and the marginalized. Finally, instruction is within easy reach; most boxing gyms are located in poor neighborhoods, where a premium is placed on being able to fight well. Male fighting is a useful skill in a cruel, frontierlike world that values physical toughness, where insult is not casually tolerated and honor is a highly sensitive point.

Black dominance in football and basketball is not simply related to getting out of the ghetto through hard work or to lack of other amusements but to the institution most readily available to blacks in the inner city that enables them to use athletics to get out. Ironically, that institution is the same one that fails more often than it should in fitting them for other professions, namely, school. As William Washington, the father of a black tennis family, perceptively pointed out in his *New York Times* article, which discussed the rise of tennis star Venus Williams, "Tennis, unlike baseball, basketball or football, is not a team sport. It is a family sport. Your immediate family is your primary supporting cast, not your teammates or the players in the locker room. . . . The experiences [of alienation and racism] start soon after you realize that if you play this game, you must leave your neighborhood and join the country club bunch. You don't belong to that group, and they let you know it in a variety of ways, so you go in, compete and leave." In short, because their families generally lack the resources and connections, indeed, because, as scholars such as V. P. Franklin have pointed out, black families cannot provide their members the cultural capital that white and Asian families can, blacks are at a disadvantage to compete in sports where school is not crucial in providing instruction and serving as an organizational setting for competition. When it comes to football and basketball, however, where going to school is essential to enabling one to have a career, not only are these sports played at even the poorest black high schools but they are also the dominant college sports. If baseball were a more dominant college sport and if there were no minor leagues where a player had to toil for several years before, possibly, getting a crack at the major leagues, then I think baseball would attract more young black men. Because baseball, historically, was not a game that was invented by a school or became deeply associated with schools or education, blacks could learn it, during the days when they were banned from competition with white professionals, only by forming their own leagues. Sports, whatever one might think of their worth as activities, are extremely important in understanding blacks' relationship to secular institutions and secular, nonprotest organizing: the school, both black and white; the independent, nonprofessional or semiprofessional league; and the barnstorming, independent team, set up by both whites and blacks.

Given that blacks are overrepresented in the most popular sports and that young black men are more likely than young white men to consider athletics as a career, there has been much commentary about whether sports are bad for blacks. The March 24, 1997, issue of *U.S. News & World Report* ran a cover story titled "Are Pro Sports Bad for Black Youth?" In February 1997 Germanic languages scholar John Hoberman published, to much bitter controversy, *Darwin's Athletes: How Sport Has Damaged Black America and Preserved the Myth of Race. The Journal of African American Men,* an academic journal, not only published a special double issue on black men and sports in its Fall 1996–Winter 1997 edition but featured an article in its Winter 1995–1996 edition titled "The Black Student Athlete: The Colonized Black Body," by Billy Hawkins. While there are great distinctions to be made among these works, there is an argument about sports being damaging to blacks that tends either toward a radical Left position on sports or, in Hawkins's case, toward a militant cultural nationalism with Marxist implications.

First, Hoberman and Hawkins have made the analogy that sports are a form of slavery or blatant political and economic oppression. Superficially this argument was made by discussing the rhetoric of team sports (a player is the "property" of his team, or, in boxing, of his manager; he can be traded or "sold" to another team). Since most relationships in popular culture industries are described in this way— Hollywood studios have "properties," have sold and swapped actors, especially in the old days of studio ascendancy, and the like—usually what critics who make this point are aiming at is a thorough denunciation of popular culture as a form of "exploitation" and "degradation." The leftist critic condemns sports as a fraudulent expression of the heroic and the skilled in capitalist culture. The cultural nationalist critic condemns sports as an explicit expression of the grasping greed of white capitalist culture to subjugate people as raw resources.

On a more sophisticated level, the slavery analogy is used to describe sports structurally: the way audiences are lured to sports as a false spectacle, and the way players are controlled mentally and physically by white male authority, their lack of access to the free-market worth of their labor. (This latter point is made particularly about college players, since the breaking of the reserve clause in baseball, not by court decision but by union action, has so radically changed the status and so wildly inflated the salaries of many professional team players, regardless of sport.) Probably the most influential commentator to make this analogy of sport to slavery was Harry Edwards in his 1969 book *The Revolt of the Black Athlete*. Richard Lapchick, in his 1984 book *Broken Promises: Racism in American Sports*, extends Edwards's premises. Edwards is the only black writer on sports that Hoberman admires. And Edwards is also cited by Hawkins. How convincing any of this is has much to do with how willing one is to be convinced, as is the case with many highly polemical arguments. For instance, to take up Hawkins's piece, are black athletes more colonized, more exploited, as laborers at the university than, say, graduate students and adjunct faculty, who teach the bulk of the lower-level courses at a fraction of the pay and benefits of the full-time faculty? Are black athletes at white colleges more exploited than black students generally at white schools? If the major evidence that black athletes are exploited by white schools is the high number who fail to graduate, then why, for those who adopt

Hawkins's ideological position, are black students who generally suffer high attrition rates at such schools not considered equally as exploited?

What is striking is the one analogy between slavery and team sports that is consistently overlooked. Professional sports teams operate as a cartel—that is, a group of independent entrepreneurs coming together to control an industry without giving up their independence as competitive entities—and so does the NCAA, which controls college sports, and so did the Southern planters who ran the Confederacy and controlled the agricultural industry of the South as well as both free and slave labor. The cartelization of American team sports, which so closely resembles the cartelization of the antebellum Southern planters (the behavior of both is remarkably similar), is the strongest argument to make about slavery and sports or about sports and colonization. This is what is most unnerving about American team sports as an industry, and how the power of that industry, combined with the media, threatens the very democratic values that sports supposedly endorse.

The other aspects of the sports-damage-black-America argument, principally made by Hoberman, are that blacks are more likely to be seen as merely "physical," and thus inferior, beings; that society's promotion of black sports figures comes at the expense of promoting any other type of noteworthy black person; and that black overinvestment in sports is both the cause and the result of black anti-intellectualism, itself the result of virulent white racism, meant to confine blacks to certain occupations. Implicit in Hoberman's work is his hatred of the fetishization of athletic achievement, the rigid rationalization of sports as a theory and practice. He also hates the suppression of the political nature of the athlete, and hates too both the apolitical nature of sports, mystified as transcendent legend and supported by the simplistic language of sports-writers and sports-apologist intellectuals, and the political exploitation of sports by ideologues and the powerful. As a critical theorist, Hoberman was never interested in proving this with thorough empiri-cism, and, as a result, he was attacked in a devastat-ingly effective manner by black scholars, who blew away a good number of his assertions with an un-relenting empiricism. But he got into deep trouble with black intellectuals, in the end, not for these assertions or for the mere lack of good empiricism. Hoberman, rather, has been passionately condemned for suggesting that blacks have a "sports fixation" that is tantamount to a pathology, a word that rightly distresses African Americans, reminiscent as it is of the arrogance of white social scientists, past and present, who describe blacks as some misbegotten perversion of a white middle-class norm.

There is, however, one point to be made in Hoberman's defense. Since he clearly believes high-level sports to be a debased, largely unhealthy enterprise and that the white majority suffers a sports obsession, he would naturally think that blacks, as a relatively powerless minority and as the principal minority connected to sports, would be especially damaged by it. The black intellectual who most influenced Hoberman was Ralph Ellison; and, as Darryl Scott pointed out in a brilliant analysis delivered at a sports conference at New York University that dealt almost exclusively with Hoberman's book, Ellison might rightly be characterized as a "pathologist" and an "individualist." But he was, as Scott argued, "a pathologist who opposed pathology as part of the racial debate." Yet one of the most compelling scenes in *Invisible Man* is the Battle Royal, a surreal perversion of a sports competition in which blacks fight one another for the amusement of powerful whites. Although racism compelled blacks to participate in this contest, the characters came willingly, with the winner having taken even an individualistic pride in it. Such participation in one's own degradation can be described as a pathology. How can an Ellison disciple avoid pathology as part of the debate when Ellison made it so intricately serve the artistic and political needs of his novel? Ellison may have loved jazz, and growing up black and poor in Oklahoma may have been as richly stimulating as any life, just as going to Tuskegee may have been the same as going to Harvard—at least according to Ellison's mythologizing of his own life—but he found black literature generally inadequate as art and thought that blacks used race as a cover to avoid engaging the issues of life fully. For Ellison, black people, like most oppressed minorities, intensely provincialized themselves.

This is not to say that Hoberman is justified in adding his own pathologizing to the mix, but his reasoning seems to be something like this: If racism is a major pathology and if we live in a racist society, then one might reasonably suspect the victims of racism to be at least as pathologized by it as the perpetrators. If the victims are not pathologized at all by it, then why single out racism as a particularly heinous crime? It would, in that instance, be noth-

ing more than another banal example of man's in-
humanity to man.

In response to an article such as *Sports Illustrated's* "Whatever Happened to the White Athlete?" blacks are likely to ask: Why is it whenever
we dominate by virtue of merit a legitimate field of
endeavor, it's always seen as a problem? On the
one hand, some blacks are probably willing to take
the view expressed in Steve Sailer's August 12, 1996,
essay in *National Review*, "Great Black Hopes," in
which he argues that black achievement in sports
serves very practical ends, giving African Americans a cultural and market niche, and that far from
indicating a lack of intelligence, blacks' dominance
in some sports reveals a highly specialized intelligence, what he calls "creative improvisation and
on-the-fly interpersonal decision making," which
also explains "black dominance in jazz, running
with the football, rap, dance, trash talking, preach-
ing, and oratory." I suppose it might be said from
this that blacks have fast-twitch brain cells. In any
case blacks had already been conceded these
gifts by whites in earlier displays of condescension.
But black sports dominance is no small thing to
blacks because, as they deeply know, to win is to
be human.

On the other hand, what the *Sports Illustrated* article stated most tellingly was that while young whites admire black athletic figures, they are afraid to play sports that blacks dominate, another example of whites leaving the neighborhood when blacks move in. This white "double consciousness"—to admire blacks for their skills but to fear their presence in a situation where blacks might predominate—is a modern-day reflection of the contradiction, historically, that has produced our racially stratified society. To be white can be partly defined as not only the fear of not being white but the fear of being *at the mercy* of those who are not white. Whiteness and blackness in this respect cease to be identities and become the personifications not of stereotypes alone but of taboos, of prohibitions. Sports, like all of popular culture, become the theater where the taboos are simultaneously smashed and reinforced, where one is liberated from them while conforming to them. Sports are not an idealization of ourselves but a reflection.

THE PRINCE AND HIS KINGDOM

Arguably the most popular and, undoubtedly, one of the most skilled boxers in the world at the turn of the twenty-first century was the featherweight champion Prince Naseem Hamed of England. (The "Prince" title is a bit of Platonic self-romanticism; Hamed, of lower-middle-class origin—his father was a corner-store grocer—has no blood tie to any aristocracy.) When he was a boy, Hamed and his brothers regularly fought in the streets, usually against white kids who called them "Paki." "I'd always turn around and say, 'Listen, I'm Arab me, not Pakistani,'" said Hamed in an interview. "They'd turn round and say you're all the same." Indeed, Hamed was discovered by Brendan Ingle, his Irish manager, fighting three bigger white boys in a Sheffield schoolyard and holding his own very well. The fight was probably instigated by racial insult. Although his parents were from Yemen and Naseem was worshipped nearly as a god among the Yemeni, he was actually born in Sheffield, was a British citizen, never lived in Yemen and, despite his Islamic religious practices, seemed thoroughly British in speech, taste, and cultural inclination. Yet when he was fighting as an amateur, he was sometimes taunted racially by the crowd: "Get the black bastard." Even as a professional he was sometimes called "Paki bastard" and "nigger." He was once showered with spit by a hostile white audience. But Hamed was far more inspired than frightened by these eruptions, and he was especially impressive in winning fights when he was held in racial contempt by the audience, as he would wickedly punish his opponents. For Hamed these fights particularly became opportunities to rub white Anglo faces in the dirt, to beat them smugly while they hysterically asserted their own vanquished superiority. But his defiance, through his athleticism, became an ironic form of assimilation. He was probably the most loved Arab in England, and far and away the most popular boxer there. As he said, "When you're doing well, everyone wants to be your friend."

On the whole, these displays of racism at a sporting event need to be placed in perspective, for what seems a straightforward exhibition of racialist prejudice and Anglo arrogance is a bit more complex. And a deeper understanding of the Hamed phenomenon might give us another way to approach the entangled subject of race and sports.

It must be remembered that professional boxing has been and remains a sport that blatantly, sometimes crudely, exploits racial and ethnic differences. Most people know the phrase "Great White Hope," created during the reign (1908–1915) of the first black heavyweight boxing champion, Jack Johnson, when a white sporting public that had, at first, supported him turned against him in part because he flaunted his sexual affairs with white women and in part because he seemed to be so far superior to the white opponent, Tommy Burns, from whom he won the title. The advent of Johnson did not, by any means, invent the intersection of race and sports but surely heightened it as a form of national obsession, a dark convulsion in an incipient American popular culture. The expression "Great White Hope" is still used today, in boxing, track and field, and professional basketball, whenever a white emerges as a potential star.

But ethnicity and racialism in boxing have a more intricate history than white against black. Boxers have often come from racially and ethnically mixed working-class urban environments where they fought racial insults as street toughs. This was particularly true of white ethnic fighters—those of Jewish, Italian, and Irish origin—in the United States from the turn of the century to approximately the fifties, when public policy changes widened economic and educational opportunities, and suburbanization altered white ethnic urban neighborhoods, changing the character of boxing and big-city life.

John Sullivan, the last great bare-knuckle champion, may have been "white" when he drew the color line and refused to fight the great black heavyweight Peter Jackson (at nearly the same time Cap Anson refused to play against blacks in baseball, precipitating a near-sixty-year ban on blacks in professional baseball), but to his audience he was not merely white but Irish. Benny Leonard was not just a white fighter but a Jewish fighter. Rocky Graziano was not merely a white fighter but an Italian fighter. Muhammad Ali, reinventing himself ethnically when the fight game became almost exclusively black and Latino, was not just a black fighter but a militant black Muslim fighter. Fighters, generally, as part of the show, tend to take on explicit ethnic and racial identities in the ring. One need not be a deconstructionist to understand that race *aspires* to be a kind of performance, just as athletic performance aspires to be something racial. This is clear to anyone who has seriously watched more than, say, a half dozen boxing matches. Today basketball is a "black" game not only because blacks dominate it but because they have developed a style of play that is very different from the style when whites dominated the pro game back in the fifties. It is said by scholars, writers, and former players that Negro League baseball was different from white baseball, and that when Jackie Robinson broke the color line, he introduced a different way of playing the game, with more emphasis on speed and aggressive base running. In the realm of sports, this type of innovation becomes more than just performance. The political significance of race in a sporting performance is inextricably related to the fact that sports are also contests of domination and survival. It should come as no surprise that the intersection of race and sports reached its full expression at the turn of the century when social Darwinism was the rage (Charles Murray is our Herbert Spencer); when sports, imitating the rampant industrialism of the day, became a highly, if arbitrarily, rationalized system; when business culture first began to assimilate the values of sports; when it was believed that blacks would die out in direct competition with whites because they were so inferior; and when Euro-American imperialism—race as the dramaturgy of dominance—was in full sway.

In most respects the racialism displayed at some of Hamed's fights was rather old-fashioned. This racialism had three sources. First, the old Anglo racism was directed toward anyone nonwhite but particularly against anyone from, or perceived to be from, the Indian subcontinent. (Hamed was insulted by being called a "Paki," not an "Arab," a confusion that spoke to something specific in white British consciousness, as did the statement "They are all the same.") In short, in British boxing audiences, Anglo racism was seen as a performance of competitive dominance as well as a belief in the superiority of "whiteness."

Second was the way in which Hamed fought. "Dirty, flash, black bastard," his audience used to shout, meaning Hamed had stylish moves and was very fast but really lacked the heart and stamina to be a true boxer, and he did not have the bottom of a more "prosaic" white fighter. Hamed was derided in part because his showy, flamboyant style seemed "black," although several noted white fighters in boxing history were crafty and quick, like Willie Pep. Hamed was immodest, something the white sporting crowd dislikes in any athlete but particularly in nonwhite athletes. He fought more in the style of Sugar Ray Leonard and Muhammad Ali than in the mode of the traditional stand-up British boxer. To further complicate the ethnicity issue, it must be remembered that famous black British boxers such as Randy Turpin, John Conteh, and Frank

Bruno were very much accepted by the British sporting public because they fought in a more orthodox manner.

Third, traditional working-class ethnocentrism is a part of most boxing matches, as it is a seamless part of working-class life. Hamed called his manager "Old Irish," while Ingle called him "the little Arab." A good deal of this ethnocentrism was expressed as a kind of complex regional chauvinism. Below the glamorous championship level, boxing matches are highly local affairs. Hamed received his most racist receptions when fighting a local boy on that boy's turf. This almost always happens, regardless of ethnicity, to a "foreign" or an "alien" boxer. In international amateur competitions, Hamed himself was constantly reminded that he was "fighting for England." It is all right if Hamed was a "Paki," as long as he was "our Paki."

What we learn from the example of Hamed is that race is a form of performance or exhibition in sports that is meant, in some way, for those at the bottom, to be an act of assertion, even revolt, against how things are normally done. But also, in boxing, ethnic identities are performances of ethnic hatred. As Jacques Barzun wrote, "In hatred there [is] the sensation of strength," and it is this sensation that spurs the fighter psychologically in the ring, gives him a reason to fight a man he otherwise has no reason to harm. So it is that within the working-class ethnic's revolt there is also his capitulation to play out a role of pointless, apolitical resentment in the social order. This is why boxing is such an ugly sport—it was invented by men of the leisure class simply to bet, to make their own sort of sport their privilege, and it reduced the poor man's rightful resentment, his anger and hatred, to a form of absurd, debased, dangerous entertainment. The Hameds of the boxing world made brutality a form of athletic beauty.

POSTSCRIPT: O DEFEAT, WHERE IS THY STING?

She: Is there a way to win?
He: Well, there is a way to lose more
    slowly.
        —Jane Greer and Robert Mitchum,
            from the film *Out of the Past*
I'm a loser
And I'm not what I appear to be.
        —John Lennon and Paul McCartney,
            from the song "I'm a Loser"

It is a certainty that sports teach us about defeat and losing, for it is a far more common experience than winning. It might be suggested that in any competition there must be a winner and a loser, and so winning is just as common. But this is not true. When a baseball team wins the World Series or a college basketball team wins a national title or a tennis player wins the French Open, everyone else in the competition has lost: twenty-nine other baseball teams, sixty-three other basketball teams, and dozens of other seeded and unseeded tennis players. Surely all or nearly all have won at some point, but most sports are structured as elaborate eliminations. The aura of any sporting event or season is defeat. I am not sure sports teach either the participants or the audience how to lose well, but they certainly teach that losing is the major part of life. "A game tests, somehow, one's entire life," writes Michael Novak, and it is in this aspect that the ideological content of sports seems much like the message of the blues, and the athlete seems, despite his or her obsessive training and remarkable skill, a sort of Everyperson or Job at war, not with the gods but with the very idea of God. Sports do not mask the absurdity of life but rather ritualize it as a contest against the arbitrariness of adversity, where the pointless challenge of an equally pointless limitation, beautifully and thrillingly executed, sometimes so gorgeously as to seem a victory even in defeat, becomes the most transcendent point of all. Black people have taught all of us in the blues that to lose is to be human. Sports, on any given day, teach us the same.

My barber is a professional boxer. He fights usually as a light-heavyweight or as a cruiser-weight. He would like to fight for a championship again one day, but time is working against him. He has fought for championships in the past, though never a world title. It is difficult to succeed as a boxer if one must work another job. A day of full-time work and training simply leaves a fighter exhausted and distracted. I have seen him fight on television several times, losing to such world-class fighters as Michael Nunn and James Toney. In fact, every time I have seen him fight he has lost. He is considered "an opponent," someone used by an up-and-coming fighter to fatten his record or by an established fighter who needs a tune-up. An opponent does not make much money; some are paid as little as a few hundred dollars a fight. My barber, I guess, is paid more than that. This is the world that most boxers occupy—this small-time world of dingy arenas and gambling boats, cramped dressing rooms and little notice. It is the world that most professional athletes occupy. Of particular interest to me was his fight against Darryl Spinks for something called the MBA light-heavyweight title at the Ambassador Center in Jennings, Missouri. Spinks is the son of notorious St. Louis fighter and former heavyweight champion Leon Spinks. Spinks won a twelve-round decision, and my barber felt he was given "a hometown decision" in his own hometown, as he felt he decisively beat young Spinks. But Spinks was an up-and-coming fighter, and up-and-coming fighters win close fights. When I talked to my barber after the fight, he seemed to accept defeat with some equanimity. What upset him was that the local paper, or the local white paper, as it is seen by most blacks, the *St. Louis Post-Dispatch*, did not cover the fight. It was prominently covered by the *St. Louis American*, the city's black paper. I told him I would write a letter to the editor about that; he appreciated my concern. As things turned out, the fight was mentioned in the *Post-Dispatch* ten days later as part of a roundup of the local boxing scene. My barber's fight earned three paragraphs. It probably was not quite what he wanted, but I am sure it made him feel better. After all, a local fighter has only his reputation in his hometown to help him make a living. Nonetheless, I admired the fact that he took so well being unfairly denied something that was so important to him. Most people cannot do that.

I might quarrel a little with my good friend Stanley Crouch, who once said that the most exquisite blues statement was Jesus, crucified, asking God why he had been forsaken. It's a good line Jesus said on the old rugged cross. But for us Americans, I rather think the most deeply affecting blues statement about losing as the way it is in this life is the last line of a song we learned as children, one we sing every time we go to the park to see our favorite team: "'Cause it's one, two, three strikes you're out at the old ball game."

6

Where Have We Gone, Mr. Robinson?

AT THE HEIGHT of the civil rights movement, in 1964, Jackie Robinson published a compilation of interviews with major league players and managers about the state of integration of baseball. He concluded that the sport had achieved considerable progress. Less than two decades after Robinson became the first black player in the major leagues, African Americans made up close to 20 percent of professional baseball players. Robinson's book was aptly titled *Baseball Has Done It*.

So what would Robinson make of the relationship between the game he loved and African Americans today? He would find reasons to be encouraged: baseball has become more diversified and more international than ever, racism has considerably lessened, and there are now nearly twice as many teams as when Robinson first broke into the sport sixty years ago. But African Americans are disappearing from baseball. Blacks make up 8 percent of major league baseball players today, and only 3 percent of players on NCAA Division I baseball teams. In the days to come, sociologists and sports pundits will likely cite those figures as evidence that baseball has turned its back on Robinson's legacy. And so the questions arise: Why are there so few black ballplayers today? Should there be more?

Let's examine the second question first. The percentage of black ballplayers has declined, yet it is still roughly what blacks represent in the population as a whole. So blacks are not significantly underrepresented. In the mid-1970s, when nearly one in three major league players was black, many people, including some liberals and some blacks, complained that blacks were overrepresented. The argument was that too many blacks were being steered into sports, distorting the young black male's sense of ambition.

Many people said that blacks' overrepresentation in sports such as baseball was bad; now they say that blacks' underrepresentation is bad. So which is it? Black Americans are far more underrepresented among people who win the science Nobel Prizes, but that is rarely treated as a national crisis. Winning the Nobel Prize in Medicine would do more for the group's image than winning the MVP or Cy Young awards, which black Americans have already proven they can win.

Still, there is no denying that fewer and fewer black youths are taking up the sport. One reason commonly offered is that black neighborhoods lack the necessary equipment and facilities—bats, gloves, green fields—to train children to play. In sociology this is called deficit theory, the idea that one group does not do what another group does because it lacks the resources. Deficit theory is often used to explain the behavior of black Americans, but it is almost always wrong. If lack of green spaces and the cost of equipment explain why black Americans do not play baseball today, then how does one account for the fact that blacks played the sport and even organized their own leagues in the early twentieth century—when they had less money, less access to space because of segregation, and fewer resources and faced more rigorous racism? And blacks make up about 70 percent of players in the NFL, even though football requires just as much green space, organization, and uniforms.

The real reason black Americans do not play baseball is that they do not want to. They are not attracted to the game. Baseball has little hold on the black imagination, even though it existed as an institution in black life for many years. Among blacks baseball is not passed down from father to son or father to daughter. As sports historian Michael Mc-Cambridge points out, baseball sells itself through nostalgia—the memory of being taken to a game by one's father when one was a child. But for blacks, going back into baseball's past means recalling something called white baseball and something else called black baseball, which was meant to exist under conditions that were inferior to the white version. Even the integration of baseball, symbolized by Robinson, reminds blacks that their institutions were weak and eventually had to be abandoned. As the controversies over reparations for slavery and the Confederate flag have shown, it is difficult to sell African Americans the American past as most Americans have come to know it.

Perhaps Jackie Robinson would be disappointed to know that a relatively small number of blacks still remain drawn to the game that he transformed. But he would be far more determined that all Americans acknowledge the complicated history of race in this country and how it still continues to influence their mores and conversations. The fact that many blacks have become strangers to baseball has a lot to do with the fact that they have developed a better, clear-eyed understanding of their experience as a people. And that is something about which Jackie Robinson would be proud.

Notes

Notes

INTRODUCTION

1. Debra Shogan, *The Making of High-Performance Athletes: Discipline, Diversity, and Ethics* (Toronto: University of Toronto Press, 1999), pp. ix, 45.

2. Heroism has been associated with high-performance athletics since at least the time of the Olympic Games in Ancient Greece. In the United States, it has frequently been associated with athletics, particularly in literature written for children about athletes, going back as far as the early twentieth-century juvenile novels of Burt L. Standish, the creator of sports hero Frank Merriwell, a staple of the dime novel. More recently a series of sports biographies for juvenile readers was published by Putnam in the 1970s under the general title *Sports Hero*.

3. William C. Rhoden, *Forty Million Dollar Slaves: The Rise, Fall, and Redemption of the Black Athlete* (New York: Crown, 2006), p. x.

4. Sociologist Harry Edwards, as I point out elsewhere, was vehement in denouncing sports as a form of slavery in the early days of his career as a writer and an activist. But his views have changed over the years, and he now sees sports in a much more positive light. Consider this Edwards quotation: "We are in a diminishing age of black athletic involvement. We are disqualifying our potential athletes. The black working class has always produced the athletes, not the underclass, which tended to send kids to the military or jail. The working class was stable enough to keep their kids in school. But with globalization and technology eliminating jobs, the working class began pushing into the lower class. When that happened, the athletes would not be in school but on the street, trading team colors for gang colors, especially with the elimination of the military draft. So what institutions pick them up? The jails do. The collapse of the working class has resulted in a diminishing of the athletic pool." Quoted in Shaun Powell, *Souled Out? How Blacks Are Winning and Losing in Sports* (Champaign, IL: Human Kinetics, 2007). Powell continues, paraphrasing Edwards: "Any time an avenue to employment is pinched or closed, it's never

good for black society. Especially because, in many instances, black teenagers who compete in athletics become the first from their families to attend college and get a degree" (ibid.).

5. See John Hoberman, *Darwin's Athletes: How Sport Has Damaged Black America and Preserved the Myth of Race* (Boston, MA: Houghton-Mifflin, 1997). Many noted African American scholars of sport criticized this book and felt that it overstated its case.

6. The Barry Bonds case has been a huge sports story in the United States, as it seems to both symbolize and dramatize the American anxiety about drug taking in sports and, perhaps, drug taking in the country itself. (Americans are the highest users of prescription drugs of any nation in the world.) For more on drugs and baseball, see Will Carroll, *The Juice: The Real Story of Baseball's Drug Problem* (Chicago, IL: Ivan R. Dee, 2005), and Howard Bryant, *Juicing the Game: Drugs, Power, and the Fight for the Soul of Major League Baseball* (New York: Viking, 2005).

7. Sanderson elaborates on the use of steroids in sports and the meaning of natural and unnatural in "Barry, Barry Bad? Not So Fast; Steroids

Are Not the Only 'Performance-Enhancers' in Sports," *Chicago Tribune*, November 20, 2007, and "The Unnatural: Is It Science, Drugs, or Is It Practice, Practice, Practice?" *Chicago Tribune*, June 4, 2002.

8. Allen Guttmann, *From Ritual to Record: The Nature of Modern Sports* (New York: Columbia University Press, 1978), especially pp. 47-55.

9. It would not surprise me if such measurements begin to creep into the scholarship and criticism of the popular arts, as it seems that every humanist thinker now wishes to be a social scientist before he or she dies, and hard numbers carry the delusion of verifying claims. With all of the fantasy sports games and league memberships now available, it may still be true that every sports fan also wishes to be a capitalist before he or she dies (to paraphrase H. L. Mencken) and to actually operate a sports franchise, a strange desire that combines the American obsessions with luck and power. Now the rabid and casual can pretend to own a team which, even as fantasy, people discover is better than playing on one.

1. When Worlds Collide

The epigraph is from Roger Kahn, *The Era 1947–1957: When the Yankees, the Giants, and the Dodgers Ruled the World* (New York: Ticknor & Fields, 1993), p. 202.

1. "Jackie Robinson Pitching," *Newsweek*, August 1, 1949, pp. 18–19.
2. Paul Boyer, *By the Bomb's Early Light: American Thought and Culture at the Dawn of the Atomic Age* (Chapel Hill: University of North Carolina Press, 1994), p. 102.
3. Alonzo L. Hamby, *Man of the People: A Life of Harry S. Truman* (New York: Oxford University Press, 1995), p. 390.
4. Boyer, *By the Bomb's Early Light*, pp. 335–336.
5. These ideas were suggested by Alan Nadel, *Containment Culture: American Narratives, Postmodernism, and the Atomic Age* (Durham. NC: Duke University Press, 1995); see especially part 1, pp. 13–37.
6. Quoted in Mary L. Dudziak, *Cold War Civil Rights: Race and the Image of American Democracy* (Princeton, NJ: Princeton University Press, 2000), p. 36.
7. African American film historian Donald Bogle had little good to say about Robeson's films in Donald Bogle, *Toms, Coons, Mulattoes, Mam-*

mies, and Bucks: An Interpretative History of Blacks in American Films, 3rd ed. (Continuum: New York, 1994), pp. 94–100.

8. Quoted in Martin Bauml Duberman, *Paul Robeson* (New York: Knopf, 1988), p. 342.

9. Ibid.

10. Roger Kahn, *The Era 1947–1957: When the Yankees, the Giants, and the Dodgers Ruled the World* (New York: Ticknor and Fields, 1993), p. 200. Kahn's full account of the Robeson speech and Robinson's HUAC testimony is on pp. 198–207. Other important accounts include the following: Arnold Rampersad, *Jackie Robinson: A Biography* (New York: Knopf, 1997), pp. 210–216; Duberman, *Paul Robeson*, pp. 336–362, esp. 357–362; David Falkner, *Great Time Coming: The Life of Jackie Robinson from Baseball to Birmingham* (New York: Simon & Schuster, 1995), pp. 192–203; Dan W. Dodson, "The Paul Robeson-Jackie Robinson Saga and a Political Collision," in *The Jackie Robinson Reader*, ed. Jules Tygiel, pp. 169–188 (New York: Dutton, 1997); Carl Rowan (with Jackie Robinson), *Wait Till Next Year: The Story of Jackie Robinson* (New York: Random House, 1960), pp. 201–212.

11. Philip S. Foner, ed., *Paul Robeson Speaks* (New York: Citadel Press Book, 1978), p. 202.

12. Ibid., pp. 203–204. Jervis Anderson makes this important observation about the relationship of the black masses and their leadership that amplifies Robeson: "Nor was it ever a part of blacks' political habit to trust their leaders behind closed doors—especially when those leaders were closeted with whites." *A. Philip Randolph: A Biographical Portrait* (Berkeley: University of California Press, 1986), p. 245.

13. In an interview that appeared in a news release in May 1949, Robeson said that his remark at the Congress of the World Partisans of Peace (held in Paris) about blacks fighting against the Soviet Union "has been distorted out of all recognition." But he did not deny the spirit of what he allegedly said. Moreover, at the Rockland Palace, he clearly stated: "At the Paris Peace Conference I said it was unthinkable that the Negro people of America or elsewhere in the world could be drawn into war with the Soviet Union. I repeat it with hundred-fold emphasis. THEY WILL NOT" (emphasis in original). See Foner, *Paul Robeson Speaks*, pp. 198, 209. Arnold Rampersad, in his biography of Jackie Robinson, wrote: "Robeson's remark, as reported, was

capable of two different interpretations: either that black Americans would never fight against the USSR or that such a fight would be horribly ironic, given the history of racism in America. But the second interpretation was given short shrift; the first, with its imputation of mass treason, carried the day." See *Jackie Robinson: A Biography*, p. 212.

14. Duberman, *Paul Robeson*, pp. 342, 343.

15. Quoted in Anderson, *A. Philip Randolph*, p. 331.

16. For more on the suppression of black radicalism after World War I, see Theodore Kornweibel, *Seeing Red: Federal Campaigns against Black Militancy, 1919–1925* (Bloomington: Indiana University Press, 1998), and for an account of the use of federal power to coerce black loyalty during World War I, see Theodore Kornweibel, *"Investigate Everything": Federal Efforts to Compel Black Loyalty during World War I* (Bloomington: Indiana University Press, 2002).

17. For a full account of the March on Washington movement, see Herbert Garfinkel, *When Negroes March: The March on Washington Movement in the Organizational Politics for FEPC* (Glencoe, IL.: Free Press, 1959).

18. Anderson, *A. Philip Randolph*, p. 274.

19. Ibid., p. 276.

20. Duberman acknowledges this distinction in quoting Bayard Rustin, Randolph's second-in-command, about Randolph's opposition to black military service during the early years of the cold war, before Truman desegregated the military in 1948. See *Paul Robeson*, pp. 343–344.

21. Randolph realized the radicalism of what he was proposing. In an exchange with Senator Wayne Morse of Oregon of the Senate Armed Services Committee, Randolph said he believed his call for resistance to the draft would release "nationwide terrorism against Negroes. . . . We would be willing to absorb the violence, absorb the terrorism, to face the music and to take whatever comes." Quoted in Anderson, *A. Philip Randolph*, pp. 277, 278.

22. *To Secure These Rights: The Report of the President's Committee on Civil Rights* (Washington, DC: United States Government Printing Office, 1947), p. 6.

23. Ibid., pp. 40–41.

24. Ibid., p. 47.

25. David S. Horton, ed., *Freedom and Equality: Addresses by Harry Truman* (Columbia: University of Missouri Press, 1960), p. 6.

26. Dwight D. Eisenhower suggested much the same as Truman in his testimony before the

HUAC about African American loyalty: "Moreover, I should like gratuitously to add to this testimony that I have seen or experienced nothing since the close of hostilities that leads me to believe that our Negro population is not fully as worthy of its American citizenship as it proved itself to be on the battlefields of Europe and Africa." Quoted in Falkner, *Great Time Coming*, p. 197.

27. Michael R. Gardner, *Harry Truman and Civil Rights: Moral Courage and Political Risks* (Carbondale and Edwardsville: Southern Illinois University Press, 2002), pp. 16–18.

28. "As we have proved our loyalty to you in the past, in nursing your children, watching by the sickbed of your mothers and fathers, and often following them with tear-dimmed eyes to their graves, so in the future, in our humble way, we shall stand by you with a devotion that no foreigner can approach, ready to lay down our lives, if need be, in defence of yours, interlacing our industrial, commercial, civil, and religious life with yours in a way that shall make the interests of both races one."

See Booker T. Washington, the Atlanta Cotton States and International Exposition Speech, 1895, Booker T. Washington, *Up From Slavery*, in

Three Negro Classics, ed. John Hope Franklin,
p. 148 (New York: Avon, 1956).

29. Rampersad, *Jackie Robinson*, p. 212.

30. Robinson criticized Negro League baseball in
his article "What's Wrong with Negro League
Baseball?" which appeared in *Ebony*, June 1948.
Manley responded in "Negro Baseball Isn't
Dead!" in *Our World*, August 1948. For more of
Manley's views of Negro League baseball, see
Effa Manley, with Leon Herbert Hardwick,
Negro Baseball . . . Before Integration (Chicago,
IL: Adams Press, 1976).

31. Branch Rickey, with Robert Riger, *The American
Diamond: A Documentary of the Game of Baseball*
(New York: Simon & Schuster, 1965), p. 46.

32. "Jackie Robinson's New Honor," *New York
Times*, December 8, 1950.

33. "In 1950, and the years to come, Jack battled
with umpires over matters not simply of judgment but of ethics, in his growing belief that the
umpires, all white, were abusing their power in
order to put him in his place." See Rampersad,
Jackie Robinson, p. 229; see also Jackie Robinson,
"Now I Know Why They Boo Me!" *Look*,
January 25, 1955, pp. 22–28.

34. Doby may have been operating under a similar
sort of agreement as Robinson when he broke in

later in the summer of 1947. Doby said years later in an interview, "I remember sliding into second base and the fielder spitting tobacco juice in my face, and I just walked away. I walked away. They'd shout at you: 'You dirty black so-and-so!' There's no way to walk away from that, but I did. I didn't have a fight until 1957." See Jack Olsen, "In the Back of the Bus, Part 4: The Black Athlete," *Sports Illustrated*, July 22, 1968, p. 39.

35. Bradford W. Wright, *Comic Book Nation: The Transformation of Youth Culture in America* (Baltimore, MD: Johns Hopkins University Press, 2001), p. 155. "By conservative estimates, about 300 comic book titles published in 1950 generated an annual industry revenue of $41 million. In 1953 over 650 titles grossed $90 million. Average monthly circulation had grown from $17 million in 1940 to nearly $70 million by 1953."

36. It is ironic that the HUAC had previously attacked popular culture in its 1947 investigation of Hollywood. Now it was using a figure from popular culture (Robinson) to legitimate black loyalty and American political principles. In 1954, Congress went after popular culture again; this time the U.S. Subcommittee to Investigate Juvenile Delinquency investigated comic books.

37. Rowan, *Wait Till Next Year*, pp. 202–203, emphasis Rowan.

38. Duberman, *Paul Robeson*, pp. 282–283.

39. "The voluntary elimination of racial bans of differentials in employment practices by many business concerns, and the employment of Negro baseball players by teams in both major leagues, deserve high praise." In *To Secure These Rights*, p. 18.

40. Jackie Robinson, as told to Alfred Duckett, *I Never Had It Made: An Autobiography* (Hopewell, NJ: The Ecco Press, 1995), originally published in 1972, p. 85.

41. Rowan, *Wait Till Next Year*, p. 203, emphasis in original.

42. Robinson, *I Never Had It Made*, pp. 82, 83.

43. Rickey had read Myrdal's *An American Dilemma* and discussed it with family and friends. Myrdal probably validated Rickey's thinking about the integration of baseball. See Lee Lowenfish, *Branch Rickey: Baseball's Ferocious Gentleman* (Lincoln: University of Nebraska Press, 2007), p. 351. In most respects, Rickey was a prototypical anti-racist, anti-communist, cold war liberal. One of the qualities that most impressed Rickey when he first met Robinson was that Robinson was a Christian who understood the underlying Christian significance of what he was being asked to do in behaving in a certain way in his first three years in white professional baseball.

See Rickey, *The American Diamond*, p. 46. For more on Myrdal's impact on American race relations and white liberals in the 1940s and 1950s, see Jules Tygiel, *Baseball's Great Experiment: Jackie Robinson and His Legacy* (New York: Oxford University Press, 1993), originally published in 1983, pp. 7–9.

44. Kahn, *The Era 1947–1957*, pp. 202–203, emphasis Kahn.

45. David Falkner provides the fullest account of Stokes, who was an African American investigator for the HUAC. According to Falkner, Stokes was a Republican who worked for Congressman J. Parnell Thomas. Stokes felt it was in the interests of blacks to testify and to denounce communism, as it was simply a stigma that made being black that much worse. Robinson had been selected over Joe Louis to testify, perhaps in part because in March 1949 Louis retired. (He would make an unsuccessful comeback two years later.) This made Robinson the most famous *active* black athlete. Singer Lena Horne was eager to testify, as she wished to clear herself of any communist taint, but she was never called. Stokes thought Robeson's Paris statement tar-brushed blacks with communism, arguing that having blacks identified with communism

served the hard Left's cause, as it would make blacks even more of a pariah group. Stokes testified before the HUAC as well. See Falkner, *Great Time Coming*, pp. 184–186, 197–198, 199.

46. Sherrie Mershon and Steve Schlossman, *Foxholes and Color Lines: Desegregating the U.S. Armed Forces* (Baltimore, MD: Johns Hopkins University Press, 1998), pp. 136–138.

47. See Jules Tygiel, "The Court-Martial of Jackie Robinson," in *The Jackie Robinson Reader*, pp. 39–51; Rampersad, *Jackie Robinson*, pp. 102–109; Falkner, *Great Time Coming*, pp. 78–86; Robinson, *I Never Had It Made*, pp. 17–23.

48. Rowan, *Wait Till Next Year*, pp. 208–210.

49. Duberman, *Paul Robeson*, p. 365.

50. Veterans of the 24th Infantry complained so bitterly and so persistently about how their performance in Korea was described in popular and academic literature that the army did an official history of the unit in Korea. See William T. Bowers, William M. Hammond, and George L. MacGarrigle, *Black Soldier, White Army: The 24th Infantry Regiment in Korea* (Washington, DC: United States Army Center of Military History, 1996). Two remarkable autobiographies by African Americans in the 24th Infantry during the Korean War are Lt. Colonel Charles

M. Bussey, *Firefight at Yechon: Courage and Racism in the Korean War* (McLean, VA: Brassey's, 1991), and Curtis James Morrow, *What's a Commie Ever Done to Black People? A Korean War Memoir* (Jefferson, NC: McFarland & Company, 1997).

51. Strode provides a useful account of this role and his preparation for it in Woody Strode (with Sam Young), *Goal Dust: An Autobiography* (Lanham, MD: Madison Books, 1990), pp. 191–194. What is ironic is that Strode trained for the part with actor James Edwards who, for a time, was the most promising black film actor of the era and had appeared in, in addition to *Home of the Brave*, such 1950s war movies as *The Steel Helmet*, *Men in War*, and *Bright Victory*.

52. Rickey, *The American Diamond*, p. 47.

2. CURT FLOOD, GRATITUDE, AND THE IMAGE OF BASEBALL

The epigraph is from Jack Olsen, "The Black Athlete—A Shameful Story; Part IV: In the Back of the Bus," *Sports Illustrated*, July 22, 1968, p. 34.

1. Curt Flood, with Richard Carter, *The Way It Is* (New York: Trident Press, 1971), pp. 233–234. The

entire text of Busch's speech makes up appendix B of Flood's autobiography, pp. 228–236.

2. Ibid., p. 235.

3. Ibid., pp. 181–182

4. Bill Nunn Jr., "Change of Pace," *The New Pittsburgh Courier*, March 22, 1969.

5. Dick Allen and Tim Whitaker, *Crash: The Life and Times of Dick Allen* (New York: Ticknor and Fields, 1989), pp. 69–70.

6. For more on Allen's drinking habits, see ibid., pp. 101–103.

7. For more on Allen's tenure in Philadelphia, see Allen and Whitaker, *Crash*, and Richard Orodenker, ed., *The Phillies Reader* (Philadelphia, PA: Temple University Press, 1996), particularly the essays comprising the section "The Mauch Years." Gene Mauch was the manager of the Phillies for much of Allen's time with the team. The two men never got along well.

8. Robert Lipsyte, "Waiting for Richie," *New York Times*, March 9, 1970.

9. Stan Hochman, "Flood's Business Is Booming, Urge to Play Isn't," *Philadelphia Daily News*, November 19, 1969.

10. Allen and Whitaker, *Crash*, p. 64, emphasis added.

11. Allen actually did return to Philadelphia for the 1975 and 1976 seasons. He had announced his

retirement after his 1974 season with the Chicago White Sox but was talked into returning to Philadelphia during the off-season when Phillies third baseman Mike Schmidt, second baseman Dave Cash, and announcer and Hall of Famer Richie Ashburn descended on his home and told him how much he was needed and how much the city had changed. Allen was primarily impressed by what Ashburn told him. See Allen and Whitaker, *Crash*, pp. 153–157.

12. Harry Edwards, *The Revolt of the Black Athlete* (New York: The Free Press, 1969), p. 13.

13. Ibid., p. 24.

14. Ibid., p. 26.

15. Ibid., p. 27.

16. Ibid., pp. 25–26.

17. Ibid., p. 16.

18. Ibid., p. 22.

19. Jack Olsen, "The Black Athlete—A Shameful Story; Part IV: In the Back of the Bus," *Sports Illustrated*, July 22, 1968, p. 28.

20. Muhammad Ali, "'I'm Sorry, but I'm Through Fighting Now,'" *Esquire*, May 1970, p. 121, emphasis added.

21. "The Black Scholar Interviews Muhammad Ali," *The Black Scholar*, June 1970, p. 33.

22. For specifics on the Nation of Islam's view of sports, see founder Elijah Muhammad's *Message to the Blackman in America* (Chicago, IL: Muhammad's Temple No. 2, 1965), pp. 246–247. Also see the several references in this book to Muhammad Ali for Elijah Muhammad's views on boxing. I am reminded that Ali was suspended from the Nation of Islam in the late 1960s for expressing a desire to return to boxing. This is why he began to make statements deploring boxing as a cruel sport of slave origin.

23. See Frederick Douglass, *The Narrative of the Life of Frederick Douglass, An American Slave*, in *The Classic Slave Narratives*, ed. Henry Louis Gates, p. 299 (New York: New American Library, 1987); Richard Wright, "High Tide in Harlem: Joe Louis as a Symbol of Freedom," in *Speech and Power: The African-American Essay and Its Cultural Content from Polemics to Pulpit, Vol. 1*, ed. Gerald Early, pp. 153–157 (Hopewell, NJ: The Ecco Press, 1992). Also see, in this regard of a skeptical view of African Americans and sports among leading black intellectuals, LeRoi Jones, "The Dempsey-Liston Fight," in *Home: Social Essays*, pp. 155–160 (New York: William Morrow, 1966).

24. William C. Rhoden makes an argument like this in his *Forty Million Dollar Slaves: The Rise, Fall, and Redemption of the Black Athlete* (New York: Crown, 2006). "For black athletes in the United States, the roots of black muscle are buried in the blood-soaked plantations of Virginia, South Carolina, Mississippi, and Georgia, where the majority of slaves were first brought to America for their physical labor. The plantation is where the black athlete's dramatic march through history began" (p. 33).

25. Jack Olsen, "The Black Athlete—A Shameful Story; Part I: The Cruel Deception," *Sports Illustrated*, July 1, 1968.

26. "Needed—An Abe Lincoln of Baseball," Ebony Photo-Editorial, *Ebony*, April 1964, p. 110.

27. Ibid.

28. It was noted in the black press on more than one occasion that black baseball players were among the highest-paid athletes in sports. See, for instance, black sportswriter Wendell Smith's column, "Baseball Salaries Are Tops in Sports," *The Pittsburgh Courier*, February 10, 1962.

29. Quoted in Jack Olsen, "The Black Athlete—A Shameful Story; Part IV: In the Back of the Bus," *Sports Illustrated*, July 22, 1968, p. 34. Concern about the conservatism of black

baseball players was expressed in several Wendell
Smith columns: "Baseball Stars Can Take
Anti-Bias Tip from Cagers," *The Pittsburgh
Courier*, October 28, 1961; "Negro Players in the
Majors Have Huge Responsibility to Meet," *The
Pittsburgh Courier*, September 21, 1963; "Isn't It
About Time for Negro Athletes to be Heard from
in Civil Rights Fight?" *The Pittsburgh Courier*,
March 14, 1964.

30. Olsen, "The Black Athlete—A Shameful Story;
Part I: The Cruel Deception," p. 15.

31. Flood, *The Way It Is*, p. 15.

32. Ibid., p. 14.

33. Ibid., p. 194.

34. Ibid.

35. Ibid., p. 16.

36. Ibid., p. 18.

37. Ibid., p. 49.

38. Quoted in Richard Reeves, "The Last Angry
Men," *Esquire*, March 1, 1978, p. 42.

39. It is interesting to note that in the tangled world
of racial politics, just as African American
athletes were protesting vehemently against racial
quotas in sports, other policy makers of the
period, both black and white, and leading civil
rights advocates were creating the Philadelphia
Plan (1969) that required racial quotas in hiring

for government contractors, the policy that became known as affirmative action. In the 1970s certain racial milestones were reached in major league baseball: the Hall of Fame launched its special committee to consider and elect players, coaches, and managers from the Negro leagues to the Hall; in 1971 the first all-star game featuring starting African American pitchers (Dock Ellis of the Pittsburgh Pirates and Vida Blue of the Oakland Athletics) was played; in 1975 Frank Robinson was hired by the Cleveland Indians as the major leagues' first black manager; and in 1976 Bill Lucas became the first African American baseball executive who served as his organization's general manager. By 1975 African Americans made up 27 percent of major league players, an all-time high. How much this was a consequence of color-blind policies and color-conscious affirmative action is difficult to say.

40. Quoted in Olsen, "The Black Athlete—A Shameful Story; Part IV, p. 39.

41. Harry Edwards, *Sociology of Sports* (Homewood, IL: The Dorsey Press, 1973), p. 282.

42. Flood's inability to return after a year's layoff greatly concerned sportswriter Norman Wallace of the *St. Louis Argus*, a black newspaper:

Curt has problems . . . of some nature that [are] preventing him from returning to the baseball world and regaining the fame he once enjoyed as a member of the St. Louis Cardinals. I got to know Flood real good in the short time that our friendship developed. He was a tremendous outgoing person, the type of guy that one enjoyed being around. Some people think Curt has a woman problem. This might be true. But it is rather difficult for me to think he has a woman problem when I know of the babes who ran after him while he was here in St. Louis. But the grand centerfielder wasn't interested. Perhaps being away from his family might have some influence on his present conduct. However, I hope that Curt will get a hold of himself, cast off whatever evils are bugging him and return to the game he loves and demands the salary his abilities merit. There is no way to tell me that Curt is finished in baseball at such a young age. The man has too much natural talent and energy. Now he merely needs to exercise the determination to make the big top once again. (*St. Louis Argus*, May 7, 1971, ellipsis in original)

43. Jim Murray, "'Uncle Curt's Cabin,'" *The Sporting News*, February 7, 1970, p. 45.

44. Red Smith, "Baseball Bondage Priced at $90,000," *The Philadelphia Inquirer*, February 8, 1970.

45. Quoted in Neal Russo, "Flood Case: Is Reserve Clause Constitutional?" *St. Louis Post-Dispatch*, January 4, 1970.

46. Bill Nunn Jr. "Change of Pace," *The Pittsburgh Courier*, April 11, 1970.

47. Bill Nunn Jr. "Change of Pace," *The Pittsburgh Courier*, May 30, 1970.

48. Bill Nunn Jr., "Change of Pace," *The Pittsburgh Courier*, March 21, 1970.

49. Bayard Rustin, "In Support of Curt Flood's Anti-Trust Suit Against Baseball," *The Philadelphia Tribune*, February 17, 1970.

50. Ric Roberts, "Flood's Big Gamble," *The New Pittsburgh Courier*, February 28, 1970.

51. Jess Peters Jr., "Jess' Sports Chest," *The Pittsburgh Courier*, April 22, 1972.

52. "Found—An 'Abe Lincoln' of Baseball," Ebony Photo-Editorial, *Ebony*, March 1970, p. 110.

53. *St. Louis Post-Dispatch*, August 14, 1970.

54. *St. Louis Post-Dispatch*, January 25, 1970.

55. *St. Louis Post-Dispatch*, March 6, 1970.

56. "Does 'Principle' or 'Principal' Motivate Flood?" *St. Louis Post-Dispatch*, January 25, 1970. Actually a less affluent player did chal-

lenge the reserve clause in 1952. In *Toolson v.
the New York Yankees*, a minor leaguer sued for
his freedom to sell his services outside of the
Yankee organization. The case reached the
Supreme Court. Toolson lost. In point of fact,
the legal principles involved in deciding either
for or against the existence of the reserve clause
have nothing to do with what the plaintiff in the
case makes.

57. "Sports Get Jilted When Athletes Go A-court-
ing," *St. Louis Post-Dispatch*, March 6, 1970.

58. "$100,000 A Year—What a Way to Be Mistreated,"
St. Louis Post-Dispatch, August 14, 1970.

3. DONOVAN McNABB, RUSH LIMBAUGH, AND THE MAKING OF THE BLACK QUARTERBACK

1. Quoted in Zev Chafets, *Rush Limbaugh: An
Army of One* (New York: Sentinel, 2010), p. 179.

2. Ibid., p. 178. The political nature or implications of professional football can be more
intricate or enigmatic than might appear on
the surface. As Mark Bowden wrote in *Bringing the Heat*, about the 1992 Philadelphia
Eagles, "Pro football is a conservative game. . . .
Football attracts conservatives. Maybe it's the

martial parallel. The Game is chocked with Silverbacks, men for whom the old rules of Western culture work. Flamingly creative souls simply do not end up coaching football teams. And the Pigskin Priesthood turns already conservative men into overmentored, blindered traditionalists. Money and hype nurture this natural hidebound bent by investing every season, even every game, with such career significance for both player and coach that no one dares fail magnificently." See Bowden, *Bringing the Heat* (New York: Atlantic Monthly Press, 1994), p. 361. But Michael McCambridge provides a historical context that differs a bit from Chafets's. To be sure, Richard Nixon was a huge football fan, as McCambridge recounts his visit to the New York Giants' locker room just before the 1959 NFL championship game, shaking every player's hand and discussing briefly what sort of year he had. See McCambridge, *America's Game: The Epic Story of How Pro Football Captured a Nation* (New York: Random House, 2004), pp. 159–160. But McCambridge also goes on to talk about how John Kennedy and his brothers loved football and played rough-and-tumble games at the Hyannis Port family compound. In the late 1960s, pro football seemed to repudiate the values of the New Left, but McCambridge writes: "But it wasn't that simple. While a society was celebrating peace and love and community, the rising sport of the age did seem to espouse contradictory impulses of violence and aggression—yet simultaneously it embodied the same sense of community that fueled the counterculture movement. The very men that the left criticized for unchecked aggression and militarism were also those most able to work together toward a common goal" (pp. 245–246). Coach Vince Lombardi, arguably the most famous man in professional football during the 1960s, was admired by conservatives such as Richard Nixon and liberals such as Robert Kennedy. Among the Left, Senator Eugene McCarthy, Abbie Hoffman, and members of the Black Panthers loved football (pp. 262–263).

3. Thomas George, "McNabb Issues His Reply," *New York Times*, October 6, 2003.

4. This point is made early on in Darryl Strawberry, with John Strausbaugh, *Straw: Finding My Way* (New York: HarperCollins, 2009). The former New York Mets, Los Angeles Dodgers, and New York Yankees outfielder writes:

I'm telling [my] story now because I want other people not to have to wait as long as I did to find

the peace I've found. Why it took me so long
probably has something to do with professional
sports, where you're supposed to be strong,
always a champion. You're not supposed to hurt.
Things are not supposed to affect you. You play
and produce no matter what.

And if you do well, you're treated like a star.
You never have to grow as a man. Someone's
always there to manage your life for you. If
you have aches and pains, you call the trainers.
When it's time to negotiate a contract or do
other business, you call your agent. If you get
in some kind of trouble . . . you call your
agent again, and he calls a lawyer. You live
your life like a child, playing a game, while a
team of professionals takes care of all your
needs. (p. ix)

5. "As with all civil rights struggles, the battle to
integrate the quarterback position stirred
passions. What's unique about it is that the
debate raged on long after every other position
in the four major sports had been opened to
African-American athletes. Why? Well, no other
position requires so much of one person. Not
goalie in hockey, not point guard or center in
basketball, not pitcher or catcher in baseball. In

the hearts and minds of hard-core football fans, the quarterback is the epitome of leadership, the CEO, the true Big Man on Campus." See William C. Rhoden, *Third and a Mile: The Trials and Triumphs of the Black Quarterback* (New York: ESPN Books, 2007), p. 3.

6. "Limbaugh Quits ESPN over Furor about Remarks," *St. Louis Post-Dispatch*, October 2, 2003.

7. Richard Sandomir, "ESPN Responds, but Its Leaders Hide," *New York Times*, October 6, 2003.

8. Some of Jackson's remarks were taken from "Welcome to Rush Week," in *Sports Illustrated*, October 13, 2003.

9. Sandomir, "ESPN Responds."

10. Allen Barra, "Rush Limbaugh Was Right," *Slate*, October 2, 2003.

11. Bernie Miklasz, "McNabb's Race Is Not the Reason that He's Overrated," *St. Louis Post-Dispatch*, October 2, 2003.

12. Randall Cunningham and Steve Wartenberg, *I'm Still Scrambling* (New York: Doubleday, 1993), p. 147.

13. Bowden, *Bringing the Heat*, pp. 363–364.

14. Cunningham and Wartenberg, *I'm Still Scrambling*, p. 99.

15. Ibid., pp. 108–109.

16. Ibid., p. 100.

17. Bowden, *Bringing the Heat*, p. 10 passim; see especially pp. 345–378.

18. William C. Rhoden, "McNabb Watches and Wonders about the Future," *New York Times*, January 1, 2007.

19. Bryan Burwell, "ESPN Gets What It Deserves in Rush of Poisonous Venom," *St. Louis Post-Dispatch*, October 3, 2003.

20. Allen Barra, "Rush Limbaugh was Right," Slate .com, October 2, 2003.

21. Ibid.

22. See John Hoberman, *Darwin's Athletes: How Sport Has Damaged Black America and Preserved the Myth of Race* (Boston, MA: Houghton Mifflin, 1997). Many African American scholars disliked this book. Historian Jeffery Sammons of New York University organized a conference critiquing it shortly after it was published.

23. Rhoden, *Third and a Mile*, p. 185.

24. J. Whyatt Mondesire, "The Lawn: Justus League Forum," December 15, 2005, http://www.thejustusleague.com/lawn/index.php?showtopic=19595.

25. "Mondesire Stands By Criticism of McNabb," ESPN.com News Service, December 15, 2005.

26. Jesse Jackson, Op-Ed, *Chicago Sun-Times*, October 7, 2003.

27. Chafets, *Rush Limbaugh*, p. 185.

28. "Limbaugh Already Down One Vote," ESPN .com, October 13, 2009, http://sports.espn.go .com/nfl/news/story?id=4556315.